MILTON'S EPIC VOICE

MILTON'S EPIC VOICE

The Narrator in *Paradise Lost*

ANNE FERRY

With a new Preface

The University of Chicago Press
Chicago and London

TO DAVID

The University of Chicago Press, Chicago 60637
The University of Chicago Press, Ltd., London

© 1963, 1983 by Anne Ferry
All rights reserved. Published 1963
University of Chicago Press edition 1983
Printed in the United States of America

90 89 88 87 86 85 84 83   1 2 3 4 5

Library of Congress Cataloging in Publication Data

Ferry, Anne.
  Milton's epic voice.

  Reprint. Originally published: Cambridge, Mass.:
Harvard University Press, 1963.
  1. Milton, John, 1608–1674. Paradise lost. 2. Epic poetry,
English—History and criticism. 3. Narration (Rhetoric) 4. Point of
view (Literature) I. Title.
PR3562.F4   1983   821'.4   83–4839
ISBN 0–226–24468–7

CONTENTS

PREFACE (1983)

It is twenty-five years since I began to work on this book, twenty since it was first published. In that time there have been large changes in writing about Milton. Some of these differences are the expression of new modes of critical thinking; virtually all reflect differently perceived configurations of poetic tradition in English.

A measure of the changes in perspective that have reshaped our sense of poetic tradition and Milton's place in it is this. We would not expect a book about *Paradise Lost* written now to begin by placing its argument in the context of "the Milton controversy which has flourished in England and America for the past thirty years" (p. xi), or to claim that the very existence of such a debate "is a healthy demonstration of the poem's importance in our tradition and for our time" (p. xii). This is not to say that the issues argued in the Milton controversy initiated by T. S. Eliot and F. R. Leavis in the 1930s are now thought to have been factitious, and it is certainly not to deny their efficacy in stimulating serious critical discussion. What is true, however, is that there have been shifts in emphasis in writing about *Paradise Lost* published in the past two decades, which are simultaneously cause and effect of the fact that its towering greatness and luminous influence on later poets are — for most critics writing now — unarguable.

In 1958 the critical atmosphere was very different. It seemed, and so Mr. Leavis himself argued (in a letter to the

Times Literary Supplement of September 19, 1958), that the view of Milton's epic style as being monotonously musical at the expense of flexibility, precision, concrete sensory experience, dramatic control had not yet been satisfactorily answered. While some writers had defended Milton's poem by praising as decorously elevated and ritualistic the very characteristics attacked by Eliot and Leavis, no book had been written which explored in detail the nature and workings of Milton's epic language. When I began in 1958 to lecture about how to read *Paradise Lost,* to undergraduates and fellow teachers of them in the late Professor Reuben Bower's Humanities 6 course at Harvard University, I could find as a model only an essay published in 1935, "Milton and Bentley," by William Empson. In it he showed that the kind of attention to verbal detail which had come to be expected in critical writing about other poets could be brought to bear on *Paradise Lost.* The results suggested that Milton's epic language is a subtle instrument controlled to express a unified vision.

It is impossible to isolate single or simple reasons why for thirty years, despite Empson's example, the fundamental terms of the debate about Milton's verse remained essentially fixed, or why the shifts, once they occurred in the early 1960s, were reflected so rapidly in so many books about Milton published in the following years. It is possible, however, to speculate that the issues involved in the evaluation of Milton's style were originally too deeply grounded in the most fundamental assumptions of current criticism to be freed for exploration from new perspectives. For in Eliot's thinking, suspicion of Milton was inextricably entwined with the creation of an idiom for contemporary poetry. In the critical writings of both

Eliot and Leavis, this suspicion was involved with a revaluation of poetic tradition that would recognize the central place of Donne and the line of wit. Milton's verse seemed then to represent the furthest extreme to which poetic language could be carried from the sharp, concrete realization found in the dramatic speaking voice of Donne's lyrics. To defend that kind of poetry was to attack Milton's.

Readers now can scarcely imagine such a critical climate as the one against which Eliot and Leavis struggled, when Herrick, for instance, often occupied vastly more space in anthologies than did Donne. Because Donne's position as a great and influential figure in the central tradition of English poetry has by now long ceased to need defending, his differences from Milton are not seen as antagonisms; Milton's strengths are no longer threats. It is inconceivable that a serious critic could now argue, as Eliot did in his essay on Milton's verse of 1936, that it could only be an influence for the worse on any later poet, by carrying him in a direction away from the qualities valued in Donne's poetry. In fact, one of the richest lines of exploration in writing about Milton during the past twenty years has been that which traces his inspiration for later poets, including Eliot. Attention to the ways in which especially the Romantic poets worked to master the voice of the Miltonic bard has sharpened our awareness of the special powers of that voice. It has made us aware of the looming presence of the poet in all of Milton's verse, and of the shaping force of his language in later poetry. Much writing about *Paradise Lost* in the past twenty years has therefore differed from earlier studies of Milton in exploring (as Empson first provided the example) the detailed workings of his epic style in all its supple richness of diction, imagery, syntax, and structure.

It has differed in emphasis also in focusing more particularly on the voice which became an authoritative but liberating model for later writing.

Criticism of Milton in the last two decades has also departed from earlier writing in assimilating these new interests to the theoretical approach that stresses the location of meanings in the interpretive acts of the reader, rather than in the poem as a created object. The large implications of this theoretical position and its differences from the assumptions of *Milton's Epic Voice* are not for discussion here. What is relevant are the conclusions it has yielded about the activity of the reader in his responses to Milton's epic. This critical approach has been directed to *Paradise Lost* with especial appropriateness because the part assigned to the reader's experiences of the poem is particularly suited to describe Milton's epic. The grounds for this appropriateness consist in the special relationship created in the poem between reader and poet by the way its complexly characterized narrative voice tells its unique story. The nature of this special relationship and its involvement of the reader is the argument of *Milton's Epic Voice:*

> We are meant to remember that the events of the poem have already occurred, to us and to the poet, and that it is because of what happens in the poem, because we and all men were corrupted by the Fall, that we stand in need of a guide to correct our reading of it. The narrative voice is our guide. (p. 47)

According to my argument, the interpretive acts of the reader are in this sense the poem's meaning.

Yet the quoted statement (representative of many others in the book) differs in one very important respect from otherwise similar later formulations about the reader's involvement in *Paradise Lost*. This quotation and other statements of the argument in the book emphasize that what happens to the reader happens also to the poet; that we are in need of guidance because the Fall has darkened our eyes and the vision of all men, of whom the blind bard is representative as well as the reader. His capacity to guide us depends upon his shared humanity which is itself in need of divine illumination.

The epic invocations which describe the narrator's complex identity by the metaphors of the bird and the blind bard are discussed in the first chapter of this book in order to discover how his function in sharing and correcting the reader's responses is defined. There can, I think, be little question that the poet is said explicitly to be both fallen and inspired, and that his task as God's instrument is defined to be the performance for us of what he prays God will do for him in his fallen condition: what is dark to illumine, what is low to raise and support. In this character his rhetoric is held to be moral persuasion designed to guide and instruct readers whose need for such aid he shares. While these explicit definitions of the relationship between narrator and reader certainly cannot be assumed to be the single determination of the reader's actual responses to the voice addressing him, they are inevitably involved in them; *who* is speaking to us must influence our experience of *how* he speaks. It is a difference between this book and more recent theoretical discussions about the reader's responses to *Paradise Lost* that they tend to set aside the poem's explicit definitions of the poet's relationship to his readers when considering his modes of addressing them, especially in direct author comments on the speeches and actions of the characters.

This book argues that the narrative voice which is declared to be our guide characteristically mingles sympathy with judgment. It explores in detail many different kinds of passages spoken by the poet—not only author comments but invocations, descriptions, similes and catalogues, allegorical narratives, parodies—in the context of the dramatic action. These discussions aim to demonstrate that the narrative voice expresses throughout the poem the blind bard's shared sense of our bewilderment and loss, as well as his conviction of divine illumination which his inspired song imparts to us. This description of the narrative voice differs from recent ones which find that the poet's mode of speaking is typically to harass and rebuke us, that it is intended to make us feel angry and humiliated. Such a view that the narrator speaks in a superior and hostile way holds also that he uses rhetoric as a strategy of taunts and accusations to trick us into accepting his judgments, thus defining the relationship of narrator to reader as that of Satan to his followers.

This definition of the function and effects of the narrative voice is clearly altogether different from mine. It is also different from the poem's declared relationship of the blind bard to his fellow mortals, for whom his inspired song is to justify God's ways. In concluding that the reader's actual responses to the narrator's mode of address in this way contradict the relationship explicitly defined in the poem between the poet and the reader, these more recent readings approach from their own theoretical position a view of *Paradise Lost* argued by Eliot and Leavis in the critical vocabulary of fifty years ago.

A. F.

Cambridge, Massachusetts

ACKNOWLEDGMENTS

To Milton scholars and critics, to my teachers, colleagues, and students, the debts which I owe are greater than particular footnotes can acknowledge. The book itself is my expression of gratitude.

The first chapter of this study is revised somewhat from an essay entitled "The Bird, the Blind Bard and the Fortunate Fall" in *Reason and the Imagination*, edited by J. A. Mazzeo and published in 1962 by Columbia University Press with Routledge and Kegan Paul in honor of Professor Marjorie H. Nicolson. For her lectures and seminars, for ten years of her unfailing kindness and generous assistance, I can never adequately express my appreciation. Some of the ideas in Chapters I, IV, and V were first explored in lectures which I gave in Professor Reuben Brower's Humanities 6 course at Harvard University in 1958–1960. I owe much to the patient attention of the staff and students of that course, especially to Professor Brower and Assistant Professor Richard Poirier for their suggestions and encouragement, and to Mrs. Margery Sabin for her perceptive criticism of Chapters IV and V. For improvements in those chapters I am also indebted to William Alfred, Associate Professor of English at Harvard. A somewhat different version of Chapter II appeared in *In Defense of Reading*, edited by Professors Brower and Poirier and published in 1962 by E. P. Dutton and Company. Robert

Garis, Associate Professor of English at Wellesley College,
read the manuscript and by his fine judgments helped to ad-
just its conclusions. My husband, David Ferry, Associate Pro-
fessor of English at Wellesley College, made it possible for
me to write this book by his patience and support. Through
his generous reading and rereading of the manuscript, his
careful criticisms and illuminating responses, his enthusiasm
and sympathy, he made it a far better book than it would
otherwise have been. For its limitations, however, I am solely
responsible.

Cambridge, Massachusetts

FOREWORD

Any book written about *Paradise Lost* in this generation inevitably adds a voice to the Milton controversy which has flourished in England and America for the past thirty years, however peaceful the aims of its author, however uncontentious its tone.[1] The existence of such a controversy influences the kinds of questions a critic asks about the poem or tries to answer or to ignore, as it influences (often without their knowledge) how his readers judge the truth, the force, and the relevance of his arguments. There is nothing sinister in this influence. It seems perfectly appropriate that those of us who read *Paradise Lost* with continuing delight should ask ourselves why a number of our contemporaries whose critical writings we respect read the same poem without experiencing its pleasures. It also seems appropriate that we should seriously examine their serious objections. If we find that we cannot seek answers in the same terms in which their questions have been asked, we should try to understand why we cannot, and then seek answers to questions which seem to us truer to our experience of the poem. The existence of the Milton controversy has sharpened our attention and forced us to examine some of our own critical presuppositions. It has been a fruitful controversy, even if not of conclusions, because it has brought to Milton studies new vigor and new point, as well as new questions. The very fact that readers of Milton's epic have argued about its meaning and its merit is a healthy demonstration of the poem's importance in our tradition and for our time; we would not expect to engage in a Cowley controversy in which the meaning and merit of *Davideis* were vigorously debated.

The only danger of this critical climate is that the controversy itself should overshadow the poem, should displace it as the center of our interest, the focus of our attention. To avoid that danger, this book attempts to acknowledge the background of Milton criticism and at the same time to treat it in so far as possible as background. A reader familiar with recent criticism of Milton will recognize its many influences in these pages. He will find that a number of statements recurrent in the Milton controversy are reargued here and that disputed passages are analyzed in detail, although there is no attempt within the limits of this discussion to examine every issue debated by critics of Milton. The reader will also discover that certain relevant ideas, although perhaps more important than some other notions expanded in this book, are not elaborated here because they have been discussed at length in other works about Milton. Some repetition of ideas developed elsewhere was of course unavoidable. It was also inevitable that a study of Milton's *epic voice* should necessarily pay particular attention to narrative, descriptive, and interpretive passages — passages spoken by the narrator; monologues, dialogues, debates, interpolated histories, and prophecies spoken by the characters have been considered largely within the context of the narrator's vision.

It is hoped that the book will be intelligible as a self-contained argument to a reader who knows the poem but not

the criticism of it. Acknowledgments are given in the foot-
notes to other works on *Paradise Lost*, to admirers of Milton
whose ideas have supported and enriched my own, and to
critics of Milton whose objections to the poem have taught
me at least as much as statements with which I am more fully
in agreement.

There are doubtless a great many critical assumptions ex-
pressed in this book quite unconsciously. There are, however,
two conscious assumptions which obviously inspired the dis-
cussion and directed its nature. There is no attempt in the
book to *argue* these assumptions, but only to explore the in-
terpretations to which they can lead a reader of the poem.

The first of these assumptions is that no poem can be read
too carefully (although detailed discussion of the workings
of language requires tact and judgment like any other social
act), that it is still possible to learn more about Milton's style,
and that the only way to meet intelligent objections to *Para-
dise Lost* is to approach more closely the heart of the poem
by analysis of its language. (The term "language" is to be
understood in these pages as referring not only to "diction"
but to the combination of all expressive devices.) This book
is therefore not a historical study — although references to
Milton's background have been included when they seemed
relevant — not because of ungrateful doubts about the use-
fulness of historical investigation, but because of interest here
in another kind of critical act.

The second assumption which shapes this book is that uses
of language in poetry are in themselves interesting to talk
about, but that our final concern, our deepest interest, is in
the view of existence expressed by the language of the poem.

These essays therefore start always — as the chapter headings suggest — with analysis of some poetic device of language, but the intention at least is to analyze the style of the epic as it is designed to express the poem's meaning, and therefore to lead the discussion toward an interpretation of that meaning. The chapter headings will also reveal a large omission. The tone, imagery, diction, syntax, and structure of the poem (although these distinctions are merely conveniences of critical language) are each explored in separate though often overlapping discussions, but patterns of sound, rhythm, and meter are not analyzed separately. This omission is due only in part to diffidence about discussing technicalities of sound. It is also due to the belief that although sound and meter are interesting in themselves, and that although they contribute to the pleasure which a poem gives us independently of its meaning, at the same time as expressive devices they cannot be separated from meaning which they at once support and create, and it is as expressive devices that sound effects are relevant to this discussion of Milton's epic.

The analysis of the poem shaped by these critical assumptions has led to two large conclusions which are also not explicitly argued in the book, although the discussion is intended to show how one reader arrived at these conclusions. The first is that *Paradise Lost* is worth our continuous reinvestigation because it is a poem of the very finest order, with the power that only the greatest works of literature have to modify our ways of looking at experience, to intensify our imaginative vision, to change our lives, by the pleasure which they give us. The second conclusion is that *Paradise Lost* is a remarkable achievement of self-conscious artistry.

The more closely we study it, the more evidence we find of Milton's sophisticated mastery of style, his poetic control not only over sustained large effects, but over the minutest details of language.[2] Statements of effect in this book are not statements of intention: to say that a particular manipulation of language creates a particular effect is not necessarily to mean that Milton's consciously articulated *a priori* intention was to produce just that effect. Such conjectures of intention seem to me to be inappropriate in criticism. Yet Milton's poem makes us feel that its effects were indeed intentional. By its remarkable firmness, distinctness, and power, *Paradise Lost* makes us feel the remarkable firmness, distinctness, and power of a mortal mind illumined by immortal light. This impression is a reflection of the poem's meaning.

INTRODUCTION:
THE QUESTION
OF MEANING

Paradise Lost is the finest epic in the English language, the great poetic achievement of the seventeenth century, the fulfillment of Milton's creative imagination. In his earliest youth, as we know from the *Vacation Exercise* and the Sixth Elegy, he aspired to write an heroic poem which would equal in his native language the triumphs of Homer or Virgil or Tasso. Throughout his manhood he conceived of his life as a noble apprenticeship, a long preparation for the task of "highest hope and hardest attempting," for the role of "interpreter and relater of the best and sagest things among mine own citizens throughout this island in the mother dialect." This aim was to be achieved by "devout prayer to that Eternal Spirit" which illumines the mind and purifies the lips of the chosen prophet, by "industrious and select reading, steady observation, insight into all seemly and generous acts and affairs," and by judicious selection of a subject appropriate to its form which would be "doctrinal and exemplary to a nation." [1]

From the Cambridge manuscript in which Milton recorded notes and outlines for projected writings we know that his imagination was also stirred by the ambition to write a drama about the Fall of man, an allegorical morality play elaborating upon the story of Adam and Eve. At what time, or for what reasons, he decided to combine these two ambitions into an epic poem of man's Fall we can only conjecture. The rightness of the decision must be measured by the achievement of the poem. And the achievement of the poem must finally be measured by what in the largest sense we call its meaning.

The question of the meaning of a poem seems to me to be one question which all readers are inevitably concerned to answer. Whatever our approaches or techniques or enthusiasms may be, we are interested in discovering what the poem "is about," what vision of experience it presents, what evaluation of human attitudes and feelings is expressed by its language. Some poems may be "about" only a mood, or the feeling evoked by a pattern of sound or a color or a time of day; others may express more elaborately articulate, more systematic, or more inclusive meanings. Yet we are always concerned at some point in our experience of a poem to know what it is saying, however simple or however articulated, about the lives that human beings lead. In particular when we read *Paradise Lost* we are made to evaluate the poem's meaning from the very first lines because the epic itself claims to present a vision profoundly true and profoundly relevant to all men and to all experiences. To take the poem seriously, and of all poems it demands to be taken seriously, we must consciously attend to its meaning as we read it; our response to it must depend on its fullest vision of existence.

Milton's record of his literary intentions and theories, elaborated especially in the autobiographical passages of his prose tracts, can in some general ways help us when we seek to understand his epic. His remarks about the nature of heroic poetry are useful to us as readers of *Paradise Lost* because they reveal to us assumptions which Milton expected his readers to share with him about the kind of poem they were to read. Because no one writes epic in our time and few people read it with the sense of familiarity they feel when they read prose fiction, we have needed to be re-educated in these assumptions about heroic poetry which Milton simply took for granted in his contemporaries.[2] If we know that Milton intended his poem to be public, formal, general, ritualistic, and literary we will be less apt to seek in it the kind of personal emotions which the Romantics have taught us to associate with poetry; nor will we demand that he use the concrete, figurative, colloquial language which modern poets have learned from Shakespeare and Donne as a means of trying to objectify their feelings. Even more helpful for our understanding of *Paradise Lost*, as we shall see in some detail in later chapters, is a recognition that Milton intended his poem for an audience familiar with the particular conventions of language and attitude associated with earlier epics. Throughout his poem he calls our attention again and again, by explicit comparisons, by quotation, allusion, and parody, to the works of earlier poets. He employs self-consciously and elaborately such epic conventions as invocations, "author-comments," similes, catalogues, epithets, and repetitions, adapting the inventions of other heroic poets to the demands of his own epic. He insists that we consider his poem in relation to theirs. This relationship is one device for expressing his meaning in *Paradise Lost,* but it cannot be equated with that meaning any more than the formal theories of epic verse can explain what this particular poem "is about," what unique vision of experience its unique language expresses.

Just as some knowledge of Renaissance epic theory and the principle of literary decorum can correct certain presuppositions which might otherwise distort our reading of *Paradise Lost,* some recognition of the demands of Milton's subject may aid us in our quest for his meaning. Like all Biblical stories, the legend of the Fall of man had the authority of divine truth. It was the sacred record of events as they occurred at the origins of the divinely created world, a world in which all individual creatures and all that happens to them express meanings. Those meanings may perhaps not be apprehended by the creatures themselves, whose understandings can never be commensurate with God's knowledge, yet the inscrutability of this world is no proof that its arrangement is fortuitous. It is proof only of the limitations of the creature and the need for accommodation to those limitations in any explanation of divine meanings. Scripture itself, as an explanation of God's works and ways, provided the sacred precedent for methods of accommodation.[3] It both recorded historical truths and employed figures — metaphors, symbols, parables, allegories — to elucidate the timeless and universal meanings of those historical events. The exemplary nature of the figures in no way denied the truth of the history. By choosing the Biblical legend of man's Fall for his subject, Milton chose therefore a story associated for his readers with a special kind of language, to be analyzed in later chapters, which they were accustomed to read in special ways. Their familiarity with this sacred language, as well as their familiarity with the story itself and its accumulations of meaning in traditional Christian thought, enabled Milton to assume in his readers certain responses which, as we shall see, would aid them in their understanding of his poem's meaning.

Milton's choice of a Biblical legend for his "argument" in these general ways influenced the form and style of his poem. Yet the particular story which he chose made additional, more special demands upon his epic than would other Biblical stories which he considered as literary subjects in the Cambridge manuscript — the story of Noah, or of Samson, for example.

First, the events of his story were set in the world of prehistory. The war in Heaven, the fall of Satan, occurred before the existence of the earth; the creation of Adam and Eve and their days of innocence in Eden took place before the birth of our world of time, change, loss, and death. These events (unlike those "feignd" in the fables of pagan mythology) really occurred, Milton and his contemporaries believed, but not in precisely the ways in which events happen to us. It would therefore be impossible for us who are confined in this world by time and space to see the happenings of prehistory, mistaken to conceive of them simply in the same dimensions, as Milton recognized in an outline for the drama about the Fall of man in which he planned to have the events of prehistory related to his audience, who could not "se Adam in the state of innocence by reason of thire sin." [4] In that outline Moses was to recount the invisible

truths and in the epic of *Paradise Lost* it was also necessary
to find some means, again as we shall see an inspired nar-
rator, to envision for us what is beyond our vision.

Secondly, the story of the Fall made demands on Milton's
poem which the story of Noah or of Samson would not, be-
cause not only its events and settings but also its characters
were unique in nature. Although Milton no more believed
in the existence of Adam and Eve as mere symbols than
he believed that Noah or Samson were rhetorical inven-
tions, because Adam and Eve were the first man and woman
their story inevitably assumed unique significance. They be-
came, as their names in Hebrew signify, the representatives
of Man and Woman and their story an illustration of uni-
versal human experience. It is true that the Christian reader's
training in the multifold senses of Scripture encouraged him
to see not only Noah and Samson and all other Biblical fig-
ures, but also Ulysses or Aeneas or King Arthur as exemplary
figures and to read their stories as illustrative of general moral
truths. This practice was intensified, however, when applied
to the legend from Genesis, by the fact that Adam and Eve
were "our first parents," traditionally portrayed not as types,
like Noah and Noah's wife or Samson and Dalila, but
as archetypes in whose story we as their descendants are
uniquely involved. Milton's epic "Argument" therefore de-
manded a style at once literally convincing and appropri-
ately general, yet capable of including our own inner ex-
perience within its range of reference. This style "answer-
able" to the unique story of man's Fall will be the subject of
the following chapters.

Although the nature of Milton's story influenced the nature of his poem, the meaning of *Paradise Lost* cannot be equated with any interpretation of the Fall to be found outside the poem, with the interpretation given in Genesis itself, or in St. Paul's epistles, in patristic or reformed theology, or even in Milton's own prose. Familiarity with traditional readings of Adam's story can give us information useful in interpreting the language of the poem and, in particular, Milton's own statements about the Fall can clarify for us definitions of language used both in his poem and in his prose works. These sources of knowledge are especially helpful to modern readers, because our need to be re-educated in even the simplest theological notions and ways of thinking is perhaps still greater than our need to be re-educated in the epic tradition. An informed image of what the doctrine of the Fall meant to English Protestants of the seventeenth century and a detailed knowledge of Milton's Independent treatise *Of Christian Doctrine* can save us many blunders in our quest for the meaning of *Paradise Lost* without ever defining that meaning for us.[5]

If it is tempting to equate the meaning of the poem with Milton's prose statements about the Fall of man, it is even more tempting and at least as misleading to reduce the meaning of the epic to statements of theme given in the poem itself. The first of these statements catches our attention at the very beginning of the poem. The traditional epic invocation begins with a summary of the story and concludes with a proud declaration of the speakers' intention, which is also an announcement of the theme:

. . . What in me is dark
Illumine, what is low raise and support;
That to the highth of this great Argument
I may assert Eternal Providence,
And justifie the wayes of God to men.   (I, 22–26)

We know that we are meant to take these lines seriously;
we feel in the verse that they are given special emphasis.
They are placed at the triumphant conclusion of the prayer,
they impress us by their large abstractness of diction, and
they give an effect of firmness, almost as if they were rhymed,
because they contain a number of repeated combinations of
sounds, particularly at the ends of lines. This statement of in-
tention claims our notice and declares the seriousness of the
poem's theme. It insists that the poem "is about" a subject of
importance to all men, that it seeks to answer a question or
prove a proposition. Yet this statement is made in verse, in
a conventional form associated with epic poetry, by a nar-
rator characterized as an inspired poet who has donned his
"singing robes" to recite his vision to mankind. We must of
course consider such statements when we question the mean-
ing of *Paradise Lost*, but we must consider them as *poetic
devices* working organically with other devices of language
in the poem to express its total meaning.

To consider this opening statement in any way but as an
organic poetic device, to extract it as a definitive and inclu-
sive statement by Milton himself of the meaning of his epic
would be to conceive of *Paradise Lost* as if it were a theologi-
cal treatise like *Of Christian Doctrine*. Milton intended his
epic to answer a question or prove a proposition only in the
ways that poetry can express meanings, ways entirely differ-

ent from the abstract argumentation of his treatise. His task as a poet was not to theorize or argue but "to paint out and describe," his means the language of his poem:

> Teaching over the whole book of sanctity and virtue, through all the instances of example, with such delight to those especially of soft and delicious temper, who will not so much as look upon truth herself, unless they see her elegantly dressed . . .[6]

The "instances of example," the elegant garments of language, are the poet's ways of conveying meaning. Only by close attention to Milton's particular and special uses of language can we therefore hope to understand the vision of experience which that language was especially invented to express.

Milton's perfectly traditional notion that poetry teaches by its own delightful means, quite different from those of abstract argumentation in prose, is phrased in language which may sound archaic to us, yet it is not at all remote from our own familiar notion that a poem means more than any statement or paraphrase of its meaning can tell us. Milton's insistence that poetry teaches by pleasing example is in harmony with the modern critical assumption that a poem "acts out" its meaning as an abstract argument does not. He would agree with us that the effects of diction, syntax, imagery, sound, harmonized in an imaginative structure, create a world of people and events, ideas and sense impressions, to which we respond in a unique way and which portrays a unique view of existence, one finally irreducible to paraphrasing statement.

The assumption that a poem "acts out" rather than states its meaning has dominated modern criticism, influencing our preference for the kind of language a poem should use and our expectations about the way that language should be organized. This critical doctrine is related (perhaps as both cause and effect) to our preference for poetic diction and imagery which has sensuous immediacy and particularity, rather than the abstractness and generality of statement, and which conveys its meaning by objectifying it in some concrete image or object or situation to which the reader can directly respond, rather than by asserting it. Related also to this critical doctrine is our preference for literary structures which express their meanings by allowing them to be revealed entirely through these objective images, characters, scenes, rather than by declaration. The kind of diction, imagery, and structure which our critical beliefs have approved we have called "dramatic," and our preference has been for literature which has the apparent immediacy and objectivity of drama.

The causes for this preference are impossible to isolate, for they depend upon larger patterns of taste and therefore upon fundamental and often unanalyzed assumptions about our experience. Yet the critical language with which we habitually surround the word "dramatic" suggests some reasons why it has become one of our terms of highest literary praise.

One reason is our association of drama with demonstration. When we say that a piece of literature is "dramatic," we mean (in part) that it acts out its meanings through illustration or example rather than by statement or assertion.

Perhaps it is at once our empirical habits of mind and our disbelief in systems of absolute value which have taught us to distrust the validity or the authority of statement or assertion, to feel that they limit or distort the meaning of an experience, that language can "act out" more than it can declare. This distrust, whatever its causes, has so affected our critical judgments that many modern readers are no longer able to respond to literature of statement, suspecting it inevitably to be dogmatic or complacent or sentimental.[7]

Another reason for this preference is our association of dramatic language with psychological experience. Because this sensory, immediate, particular language intends to imitate individual thoughts and emotions, it has seemed best suited to explore or expose men's innermost experiences, those feelings which we perhaps cannot articulate or explain, which we often do not know about in ourselves, but which are the buried sources both for our behavior and for our articulated attitudes. It is these profound sources of experience which interest us and which we feel should be the concern of literature; language not devoted in some way to acknowledging these depths of experience seems to us to be dead or shallow or merely decorative.

These critical assumptions and preferences, which have dominated modern criticism, have been applied to *Paradise Lost* in very specific and special ways. The earliest group of Milton's defenders in this century, trying to combat the notion that *Paradise Lost* was a mere versification of Genesis or a Puritan tract in blank verse, insisted that the poem expresses a large and humane view of existence and that it does so by means appropriate not to theology but to dra-

matic literature.[8] Later critics, defending Milton's epic against
the objections that his diction and imagery lacked the dra-
matic particularity of Donne's or Shakespeare's, that his
poetic structure lacked the dramatic immediacy of Dante's,
have continued to emphasize the "dramatic" qualities of
Paradise Lost without always feeling the necessity to identify
which of the many definitions of the term is intended. Both
the opponents and the defenders of Milton, therefore, have
apparently shared the modern assumption that a work of
literature ought to be dramatic.

The very fact that the emphasis on the dramatic has grown
out of our most fundamental critical presuppositions has
made it a useful approach to *Paradise Lost,* more useful for
our time than some other critical approaches perhaps more
explicit and applied with a greater degree of disengagement
but more peripheral to our deepest concerns. The assump-
tions of any age of course determine its ways of reading a
work of literature, which is the most obvious reason why a
poem is reread and reinterpreted by successive generations.
The critics writing after Milton's death, for example, Dryden,
then Addison and later Johnson, read *Paradise Lost* in the
light of their own critical presuppositions. They habitually
measured the achievement of *Paradise Lost* against their defi-
nition of epic as a conventional formal presentation in lofty
verse of an explicitly stated heroic theme, judging its struc-
ture and style and meaning against their notions of an ideal
epic poem. Many of their presuppositions were shared by
Milton and certainly their approach produced some illumi-
nating observations, but it is a critical procedure which seems
to us somewhat mechanical and arbitrary, directing our at-

tention to external criteria rather than to the heart of the poem. Or when we read, for example, Addison's remarks about the theme of *Paradise Lost*, his confident assertion that its meaning can be summed up in the statement *"that Obedience to the Will of God makes men happy, and that Disobedience makes them miserable,"* [9] we perhaps feel him to be guilty of the dogmatism or complacency which make such reductive statements suspect to us. We feel the poem to be "about" more than it announces, to express a richer vision of experience than any single paraphrase can bear. And if we feel this, we feel it to have certain qualities which we may perhaps in the widest sense call "dramatic," and which make the poem moving to us as an exploration of our most deeply inward experiences.

There are of course additional encouragements for this critical emphasis inherent in Milton's own writings. He was himself always interested in the drama — attended plays or read them, wrote in praise of Shakespeare and Jonson, speculated about ancient and Renaissance dramatic theory, wrote *Arcades* and *Comus* to be acted, *Samson Agonistes* to be read as a dramatic work. The fact that he long considered the possibility of a play about the Fall of man, the elaborateness of the plans for such a work in the Cambridge manuscript, and his nephew's assertion that at least one part of the play about the Fall was actually written and then included in the later epic,[10] all encourage the notion that Milton's conception of the legend from Genesis was in some sense of the word "dramatic." Furthermore the finished epic has a large number of passages which, like dramatized scenes, are for the most part composed of speeches by characters and dialogues between them, an unusually large number for an epic in proportion to the number of lines devoted to narration, description, and interpretive comment.

The critical emphasis on the dramatic qualities of *Paradise Lost* has focused our attention especially on the actions, the speeches, and the dialogues of characters in the poem because these passages have seemed to be the most dramatic both in the simple sense that they seem to be acted out immediately before us like scenes in a play, and in the more complex sense that they seem to reveal most richly the inner lives of human beings through their discourse. Certainly such scenes — the dialogues and debate in Hell, the conversations between Adam and Eve, for example — contribute richly to our interpretation of the poem and to our pleasure as we read it. Yet if we are to understand the poem's meaning, we must remember that Milton chose to present his special subject in an epic, not a play, and that although an epic may have dramatic qualities, there are inescapable differences between the two genres which partially determine their ways of expressing meanings. These differences are not discovered by contrasting what an ideal epic should be with the rules which an ideal drama should follow, but simply by looking at the different ways in which language is made to work in the two forms, and the differences in effect which are then created. These inevitable differences must have had some influence upon Milton's change of plan.

Like a play, an epic presents a story about characters involved in events located in some identified time and place, but unlike a play, an epic must have some sort of narrator who tells the story, observes the characters, identifies the time, and describes the place. The epic is in one sense "about" the story of its characters, but that story is always presented to us in the context of the narration. This condition of epic is especially important for Milton's purposes: his story, because it is "invisible" to us, demanded not only a narrator but one endowed with unique powers of vision to make the impenetrable world of prehistory known to us. It is his voice, as we shall see, which interprets the story to us, and which is the principal device in the poem for expressing its *total* meaning.

By ignoring the role of Milton's narrator in *Paradise Lost* and concentrating instead on the speeches and actions of characters, we have in some ways allowed our critical presuppositions to mislead us. We have assumed that the meaning of the poem was to be found in our response to the characters in it as to figures in a piece of dramatic literature, whom we judge directly, by the values created in the language of the drama in relation to the values assumed in the world of the audience. But this is not the relationship in which we stand to Satan or God or Adam and Eve in *Paradise Lost*. We cannot simply respond to them directly because in the poem without the aid of the inspired narrator we could neither see nor hear them; it is his vision which determines ours and we listen only to what he recites for us. We cannot judge the characters simply by their values in relation to our own because the unfallen world of prehistory in the poem cannot be measured by mortal imaginations. We can understand that world only as it is interpreted to us by the narrator. What would appear to us true without his guidance often turns out in reality to be false, and what is acted out in the poem must always be explained by the speaker. So that when we find complexity in our response to the behavior or speech of a character and to the statement of the narrator which interprets it, we must judge the character by the interpretation, not the interpretation by the character's words or acts.

Our tendency to read *Paradise Lost* as if it were a dramatic work, ignoring the omnipresence of the narrator, has not only encouraged us to seek the poem's meaning in our direct response to characters. It has encouraged us to think of the narrator's interpretive statements as superfluities, irrelevancies, or just clumsy mistakes. The prejudice for dramatic presentation rather than interpretive statement has at least partially blinded modern readers to Milton's elaborate and sustained method of narration, so that his inclusion of statements guiding or correcting our responses to characters has been attributed to Milton's nervousness about his presentation. The assumption that poetry which demonstrates is somehow truer and better than poetry which works by statement has led to the conclusion that the poet included statements interpreting his story to us in order to prevent its dramatic passages from endangering his conscious intention, that these statements are therefore external to the organic unity and life of the poem.[11] Such an assumption has led some readers to ignore interpretive comments in the poem, others to condemn them by their very nature as comments, attitudes which seem to me to violate the poem as much as the opposite habit of equating statements in the poem with its final meaning.

Throughout *Paradise Lost* we find statements by the narrator which at least in part contradict the impression made immediately upon us by the actions or speeches of the characters. These apparent contradictions must of course be explained, if we are to be satisfied with our reading of the poem, but they can only be explained in their total context, as we shall see, by close analysis of the language of the scene. The mere presence of such statements, even their partial contradiction of some other impressions made by the language, is no sign of Milton's failure to master the techniques of narrative poetry.

Nor is it evidence that Milton's unconscious sympathies in the poem are at variance with his conscious intention. The notion that Milton did not quite know what he was doing in *Paradise Lost* is as old as Blake's famous remarks about the poem,[12] and the form in which the idea revived in this century is as much the result of our presuppositions as Blake's theory was originally the expression of his personal religion. Again it seems to me that we have misconstrued the poem by ignoring the role of the narrative voice, so elaborately created and carefully sustained throughout the poem. No piece of literature seems to me to give a stronger impression of conscious control, deliberate artistry, and carefully articulated method. Over and over again in the poem we shall find Milton calling attention to the identity of the voice, its relation to the events of the poem and to the experience of its readers. He makes use repeatedly of elaborate devices to keep us continually aware of the role of the narrator as interpreter to us of the poem's meaning.

This impression of conscious artistry in the poem is intensified by the narrator's repeated allusions to his own style. Just as the angel Raphael at intervals in his story reminds his listener, Adam, that he is using a language of accommodation to make heavenly truths visible to earthly imagination, the narrative voice elsewhere in the poem reminds us that he too is using devices of language which we must recognize if we are to understand his meaning. He claims to speak in a style "adventurous," "unattempted," which will surpass the achievements of other epic poets:

> If answerable style I can obtaine
> Of my Celestial Patroness, who deignes
> Her nightly visitation unimplor'd,
> And dictates to me slumbring, or inspires
> Easie my unpremeditated Verse . . .   (IX, 20–24)

The style itself is a miracle like the heavenly inspiration breathed into the poet. It is "unpremeditated" not because it is unconscious, but because it is mysterious, more than human, a gift of grace. We are meant to be aware of it, to feel its intensity, its uniqueness, its mystery, because these qualities express the poem's meaning. There may be some passages in which the style fails to achieve its effects, passages in which we feel its strangeness has become mechanical or merely dull,[18] but it is a style beautifully designed for its special purposes, beautifully appropriate to its special speaker. It is my belief that if we analyze carefully the nature of that speaker and the language which he uses, we will find that there is no confusion between unconscious emphasis and conscious intention, between the "dramatic" and the narrative portions of the poem. By analyzing the quality of the voice we hear in the poem, its relation to the story and to its readers, we shall be led to the heart of the epic, to the meaning of the narrator's vision.

The question of meaning will therefore be approached in this book by the question "What is the poem like?" In attempting to answer that question the following chapters will be devoted to analyzing how language works in the poem, what effects it creates, what responses it evokes in us. The description of what the poem "is like" will attempt to show, rather than the recurrence of a particular theme, some of the fullness of meaning in particular passages which have seemed to me especially illuminating or representative, and to consider these particular expressions of meaning in the context of the total vision expressed by the poem.

I · TONE – THE BIRD
AND THE BLIND BARD

The demands of narrative immediately forced themselves upon Milton as soon as he decided to present the Fall of man in an epic rather than in a play. He was consciously concerned with distinctions among literary types, as numerous prose statements show, and in *Paradise Lost* in particular he reminds us repeatedly of the deliberateness of his choice of epic form as well as of Biblical argument. He also reminds us of the consciousness of his artistry, the care with which he has sought a style "answerable" to the traditional epic form and to his special "higher Argument" (IX, 1–47). This choice of "answerable style" involved him immediately in the choice of speaker, in the problems of creating a distinctive voice capable of narrating and interpreting his argument. The narrative voice is as deliberate an invention as the other characters in the poem and essential to its meaning. For everything which is not actually *said* by this narrator — the speeches of the characters to themselves or to one another — is reported and interpreted by him, and therefore only when we have determined who is speaking in the narrative, descriptive, and discursive passages, and to whom, can we evaluate the mood and meaning of the poem.

The necessity for these questions about the narrative voice

has been obscured by the habit in criticism of referring to the speaker in the poem as "Milton." In *Paradise Lost* Milton's narrator speaks in the role of author (as the narrative voice in an epic was traditionally expected to speak), but the role of author is also conventionally assumed, for example, in the *Nativity Ode*, in *Lycidas*, and in Sonnet XII on *Tetrachordon*. All these speakers might with equal justice and equal vagueness be called "Milton"; yet our experiences of the sonnet, the pastoral elegy, the ode, and the epic are experiences of totally different voices, each speaking in the role of author.

Nor is it a sufficient explanation to say that every literary genre automatically dictated its particular kind of voice; that decorum demanded the narrator of an epic to be not only a poet but a poet reciting great actions to a large audience in a ritualistic and elevated style capable of carrying the story forward in large units of verse. It is helpful and necessary to recognize the principle of decorum at work in Milton's epic, but that principle alone does not define for us the distinctive quality of the narrative voice. For Spenser's Renaissance epic decorum dictated the same general rules, and yet the speaker in *The Faerie Queene* never sounds like Milton's nor bears at any time the relation to his audience or to the events of his poem that Milton sustains in the tone of the narrative voice throughout *Paradise Lost*.

The passages especially devoted to creating and defining this voice are those at the beginnings of Books I, III, VII, and IX, in which Milton adapts the conventional device of the epic introduction. It is precisely these passages which Addison and Johnson called "digressions" or beautiful "superfluities"; yet they are as essential to the structure and meaning of the epic as the so-called "digressions" in *Lycidas* are now generally considered to be integral to its total design.[1] To understand the complex nature of the narrative voice and its complex relation both to argument and to reader, it is necessary to analyze a number of these passages in detail. They will be seen to create and define a speaker whose identity and characteristic tone are sustained throughout the epic and control our interpretation of its meaning.

Milton's epic opens with a traditional statement of story and theme, given in the conventional form of an invocation, which sets the elevated pitch demanded of an epic style:

> Of Mans First Disobedience, and the Fruit
> Of that Forbidden Tree, whose mortal tast
> Brought Death into the World, and all our woe,
> With loss of *Eden*, till one greater Man
> Restore us, and regain the blissful Seat,
> Sing Heav'nly Muse . . .   (I, 1–6)

Although convention dictated this announcement, the speaker assumes our familiarity with the story, assumes that we can identify "*that* Forbidden Tree" and "*one* greater Man." His purpose in these lines is therefore not so much to familiarize us with the events to come as it is to identify for us which story we are to hear, what it means to us, and who is to tell it. We the readers are immediately included in the events of the narrative with the first line of the poem, because its subject is "Mans First Disobedience" (not "Adam's" or "the first man's") and in any context in which the word is used, we are included in "Man." We and the speaker are even more explicitly included in the poem's story when we are told that the Fall brought "all *our* woe" until Christ "Restore *us*." We are the heirs of Adam; it is to us and to the poet that Adam speaks directly when after his Fall he laments his legacy of corruption:

> . . . Fair Patrimonie
> That I must leave ye, Sons: O were I able
> To waste it all my self, and leave ye none!
> So disinherited how would ye bless
> Me now your Curse!   (X, 818–822)

We are never identified as "Knights and Ladies," titles which Spenser's narrator sometimes gives to his readers, nor as Englishmen or Puritans or citizens of the late seventeenth century. We are human beings, simply, and yet certain assumptions are implied about us *as* human beings. It is assumed that we loathe sin and love virtue, regret the loss of Eden and long for our restoration; that we can respond to divinely inspired music, that we are interested in the serious treatment of a serious subject, and that we are capable of rational attention to logical argument. Yet it is simultaneously assumed that as human beings we need divine inspiration because our minds cannot transcend the limits of our creaturely nature, and that as heirs of Adam we are fallen, bereft, miserable, and mortal.

The first epic introduction therefore establishes who we are as readers and what is our relation to the poet whose song we are to hear and understand. It tells us that not only are we to hear a story familiar to us, but one which in a sense happens to us and to the poet narrating it. We will at least partially share his angle of vision because we share his humanity, and more specifically his fallen nature. Like us, the speaker is at once dignified but limited because he is human, corrupted and disinherited because he is fallen.

Yet even in the introduction to Book I we feel the identity of the narrator and his relation to us to be more complex than the fact of our common nature and condition would imply. Although we may in part share the narrator's point of view, we hear no easy intimacy in these lines. The diction is formal and general, the sound sonorous, the syntax remote from speech. The speaker pictures himself as a bird "That with no middle flight intends to soar" (I, 14) in pursuit of a vision of "Things unattempted yet in Prose or Rhime" (I, 16). He assumes the more than human authority to "assert" God's Providence and even to "justifie" his ways to "men" (I, 25–26). Here the word "men" includes us, the readers, as did the earlier word "Man," and it is to us that the narrator is to explain God's ways. He is therefore not only one of "us" because he shares "our woe"; he is also apart from us, instructing us in his role as poet. The source of his vision is the same divine spirit which inspired Moses to sing of the Creation or which flowed in Siloa's brook, whose waters purged the vision of the blind man.[2] The fallen narrator prays to this spirit in his invocation, and, the prayer being granted, he can see "Above th' *Aonian* Mount" (I, 15), the imaginations of mortal poets. As inspired poet-prophet, the narrative voice claims the instruction granted to Moses and the illumination granted the blind man. He can interpret to us Adam's story and our own share in it because, like a bird, he can soar beyond the limits of our mortal experience and our fallen vision.

It is this speaker who penetrates for us the "darkness visible" of Hell and the "Illimitable Ocean" of Chaos, guiding us to the verge of the lighted world and in Book III transporting us to Heaven. The invocation to light which opens Book III not only provides a transition from one world to another. Its most important function is to reinforce and elaborate the character of the narrative voice created in the introduction to Book I.

After the opening lines of invocation to light, the speaker develops the metaphors used first in Book I to express his nature and his relation to reader and argument:

> Thee I re-visit now with bolder wing,
> Escap't the *Stygian* Pool, though long detain'd
> In that obscure sojourn, while in my flight
> Through utter and through middle darkness borne
> With other notes then to th' *Orphean* Lyre
> I sung of *Chaos* and *Eternal Night*,
> Taught by the heav'nly Muse to venture down
> The dark descent and up to reascend,
> Though hard and rare . . .   (III, 13–21)

The bird in this context is a metaphor for the narrator's double nature. Because a bird is a creature — mortal and limited — and because its song can have moral meaning only if that meaning is endowed from a source outside itself, the bird can be a metaphor, (a part as we shall see of an elaborate pattern of metaphors) for the speaker as fallen man, whose song must be inspired by the "heav'nly Muse." But because a bird is the only mortal creature who can soar above the limits of man's experience and beyond the clouds obscuring his vision, the bird can serve also as a metaphor for the speaker as inspired seer, whose song has the divine authority of prophecy. The pattern of these lines, the descent and reascent of the bird's flight, (made more terrible by its associations with the visits of Orpheus and Aeneas to the underworld) recalls the pattern of loss and restoration in the first lines of the poem, which included in their circular syntax the history of Adam and of mankind, of the reader and of the narrator.

In the next passage of the introduction to Book III, Milton develops his second and parallel metaphor for expressing the nature of the narrative voice. Here the image shifts from the speaker as bird to the more important, more elaborate, and more moving metaphor of the narrator as blind bard:

> . . . thee I revisit safe,
> And feel thy sovran vital Lamp; but thou
> Revisit'st not these eyes, that rowle in vain
> To find thy piercing ray, and find no dawn;
> So thick a drop serene hath quencht thir Orbs,
> Or dim suffusion veild. Yet not the more
> Cease I to wander where the Muses haunt
> Cleer Spring, or shadie Grove, or Sunnie Hill,
> Smit with the love of sacred song; but chief
> Thee *Sion* and the flowrie Brooks beneath
> That wash thy hallowd feet, and warbling flow,
> Nightly I visit: nor somtimes forget
> Those other two equal'd with me in Fate,
> So were I equal'd with them in renown,
> Blind *Thamyris* and blind *Mæonides*,
> And *Tiresias* and *Phineus* Prophets old.   (III, 21–36)

In these lines the pattern of descent and reascent, of loss

and restoration, of departure and return is interrupted. The light revisits "not" the speaker's eyes. "Dawn," the assurance of reascent, restoration, return is lost to him. His own light is "quencht," his vision "dim" and "veild"; and, like the blind poets and prophets of old, he can "find no dawn." Yet despite his loss he retains his "love of sacred song," his dedication to poetry. Like the man born blind in the Gospel according to St. John, he is marked by blindness which is not a special curse on his wickedness but a sign "that the works of God should be made manifest in him" (John ix:3). Because he is afflicted with the more than human suffering we associate with blindness, we feel him to be capable of more than human profundities of experience. Because he can no longer see the colors and surfaces of things, we feel him to have special powers of inner illumination which penetrate the veils dimming our mortal vision.

Once Milton has elaborated these two metaphors for the speaker's role — the images of the bird and blind bard — he fuses them in a single simile:

> Then feed on thoughts, that voluntarie move
> Harmonious numbers; as the wakeful Bird
> Sings darkling, and in shadiest Covert hid
> Tunes her nocturnal Note.   (III, 37–40)

When the speaker as blind poet compares himself here to a bird whose song rises in the darkness from an unseen source, Milton explicitly unifies the two metaphors as part of the total expression of the narrator's nature. The fact that Milton himself was blind must of course have partly determined his choice of metaphors, and our knowledge of that fact gives added poignancy to these lines. But the habit in criticism of referring to this and other passages about blindness as "autobiographical" (like the habit of referring to the speaker in the epic as "Milton") blurs our awareness of the metaphorical function of the lines. Like the language about birds, song, wings, flight, the language about blindness, vision, darkness, light is metaphorical here as it is in *Samson Agonistes* and indeed in *Areopagitica*, written almost a decade before Milton's own loss of sight. In one of the most famous passages of that treatise, for example, he uses the same metaphors developed in the invocation to Book III:

> Methinks I see in my mind a noble and puissant nation rousing herself like a strong man after sleep, and shaking her invincible locks: methinks I see her as an eagle mewing her mighty youth, and kindling her undazzled eyes at the full midday beam; purging and unscaling her long-abused sight at the fountain itself of heavenly radiance . . .[3]

The blind Samson redeemed by the illumination of heavenly grace and the bird soaring to the source of unshadowed light are parallel images here as in the opening of Book III. In the epic both images express the complex nature of the narrative voice — the speaker as limited human creature whose vision was dimmed by the Fall (just as Satan's brightness was eclipsed by his sin and Adam's eyes were darkened by disobedience); and the speaker as inspired seer whose divine illumination transcends the limits of mortal vision.

The way Milton exploits the metaphorical language about blindness in the remaining passage of this epic introduction is one of his most dazzling achievements. In these lines he extends the metaphors developed in the passage until they

include the total pattern of the poem — the cycle of loss
and restoration announced in the opening sentence and ex-
pressed in the mood of its final lines:

> Thus with the Year
> Seasons return, but not to me returns
> Day, or the sweet approach of Ev'n or Morn,
> Or sight of vernal bloom, or Summers Rose,
> Or flocks, or herds, or human face divine;
> But cloud in stead, and ever-during dark
> Surrounds me, from the chearful waies of men
> Cut off, and for the Book of knowledg fair
> Presented with a Universal blanc
> Of Natures works to mee expung'd and ras'd,
> And wisdome at one entrance quite shut out.
> So much the rather thou Celestial light
> Shine inward, and the mind through all her powers
> Irradiate, there plant eyes, all mist from thence
> Purge and disperse, that I may see and tell
> Of things invisible to mortal sight.   (III, 40–55)

In this passage syntax and imagery work together in two
contrasting sentences to express the double nature of the
narrative voice. The first sentence is extended for ten lines
through a long list of nouns, then a series of clauses and
qualifying phrases, punctuated with many pauses. The sec-
ond sentence is only five lines long, consisting of five im-
peratives contained by the end-rhymes of "light" and "sight."
The contrasting syntax of these two sentences reinforces the
contrasting images of light, and these images control the
tone in which the narrative voice interprets to us his "great
Argument," what man has lost and what he has gained.
  The images of light in the first sentence describe the light

which is now dark to the blind poet. They are images of the passing year, of the cycles of sunrise and nightfall, the seasonal changes of foliage and scenery. This simple, general, idealized language is deliberately conventional. The images of light falling on "flocks" or "herds," on the "Summers Rose" or the "vernal bloom" are obviously intended to remind us of pastoral poetry, which celebrated the pagan myth of the simpler and purer world at the origins of our history. They also refer us to passages elsewhere in *Paradise Lost* in which the narrative voice describes existence in the Garden of Eden.[4] Perhaps the most familiar of these passages is one in which the Garden is explicitly compared to the world of pastoral poetry:

> . . . Thus was this place,
> A happy rural seat of various view;
> Groves whose rich Trees wept odorous Gumms and Balme,
> Others whose fruit burnisht with Golden Rinde
> Hung amiable, *Hesperian* Fables true,
> If true, here onely, and of delicious taste:
> Betwixt them Lawns, or level Downs, and Flocks
> Grasing the tender herb, were interpos'd,
> Or palmie hilloc, or the flourie lap
> Of som irriguous Valley spread her store,
> Flours of all hue, and without Thorn the Rose . . .
>   (IV, 246–256)

Earthly Paradise is the pagan Golden Age once true, and the images in which the narrative voice describes it remind us specifically of those in the introduction to Book III. The day's cycle, from which the blind bard is cut off, here frames this first description of Eden:

            . . . the Sun
Declin'd was hasting now with prone carreer
To th' Ocean Iles, and in th' ascending Scale
Of Heav'n the Starrs that usher Evening rose . . .
                              (IV, 352–355)

The sentence in the introduction to Book III in which the
speaker as blind bard describes the changing light of the
seasons and the day refers us then to the world of the pagan
Golden Age, the world of pastoral poetry, and also to his
own descriptions of the Garden of Eden. Again and again
in the poem Eden is described in images of the rotating
light of sun, moon, and stars, and Adam and Eve both re-
peatedly sing the praises of sunrise and nightfall. To them
before the Fall, this cyclical pattern was an emblem of order,
a cycle whose constant renewal was an assurance of perma-
nence. The endless rotation of day and night told them that
nothing in nature was lost or wasted, just as we are told that
before the Fall the bower of Adam and Eve "Showrd Roses,
which the Morn repair'd" (IV, 773). But to the fallen reader
and the fallen narrator, the changing light of nature means
what it means to Adam and Eve after the Fall — that nothing
in nature is permanent, that everything vulnerable is threat-
ened and everything beautiful will fade, like the garland
that Adam weaves for Eve which, after her sin "Down
drop'd, and all the faded Roses shed" (IX, 893).

The sense of loss shared by narrator and reader from the
beginning of the epic is experienced by Adam and Eve after
the Fall, when their minds become darkened like the speak-
er's eyes, and they too are cut off from the Garden of Eden.
The blind bard's lament for his personal loss of the world of

pastoral nature is echoed by Eve when she first learns that
she must be banished from her native home in Paradise:

> O unexpected stroke, worse then of Death!
> Must I thus leave thee Paradise? thus leave
> Thee Native Soile, these happie Walks and Shades,
> Fit haunt of Gods? where I had hope to spend,
> Quiet though sad, the respit of that day
> That must be mortal to us both. O flours,
> That never will in other Climate grow,
> My early visitation, and my last
> At Eev'n, which I bred up with tender hand
> From the first op'ning bud, and gave ye Names,
> Who now shall reare ye to the Sun, or ranke
> Your Tribes, and water from th' ambrosial Fount?
> Thee lastly nuptial Bowre, by mee adornd
> With what to sight or smell was sweet; from thee
> How shall I part, and whither wander down
> Into a lower World, to this obscure
> And wilde, how shall we breath in other Aire
> Less pure, accustomed to immortal Fruits?   (IX, 268–285)

The loss of innocence is the loss of Eden, and the loss of
Eden is the loss of the pastoral world. What was true of
man's experience before the Fall has become merely a fable.[5]
Adam and Eve, like the fallen reader and the blind narrator,
are irrevocably cut off from the light of Eden, the true pat-
tern of pastoral nature, and are forced to "wander down"
into the world of chance and change, the world in which
the reader and the blind speaker now live.

Yet if we are to understand how Milton would have us
interpret their banishment and our own, we must remember
that in the epic introduction to Book III the speaker contrasts

the lost light of Eden with a different kind of light. This is the light of divine inspiration shining within the purified heart of the blind bard, the light which is granted to him as fallen man when he prays for divine illumination to purge the mists obscuring his vision. It is a steadier light than the changing light of nature and it enables the blind bard to see beyond the colors and surfaces of things. It is a celestial, not a mortal light. It can "plant eyes" (III, 53), and the metaphor implied by the verb "plant," with its connotations of organic vitality and growth, suggests a new creation of a new nature. This is the light which gives authority to the voice of the blind bard, granting him the power to "see and tell/ Of things invisible to mortal sight" (III, 53–54). It is the same illumination which is granted to Adam and Eve at the end of the poem when they come to realize that they must seek a "Paradise within" them, happier far (XII, 587). It is the light which enables Eve to see that the lost pastoral world of Eden is less precious than the Eden within the soul. In Book XII she is finally reconciled to her banishment from the pastoral world, as the speaker is reconciled to his blindness. She expresses her acceptance when she says to Adam:

> . . . but now lead on;
> In mee is no delay; with thee to goe,
> Is to stay here; without thee here to stay,
> Is to go hence unwilling; thou to mee
> Art all things under Heav'n, all places thou,
> Who for my wilful crime art banisht hence.   (XII, 614–619)

In the final passage of the epic introduction to Book III, the contrasts of syntax and imagery help to create the complex

tone which characterizes the narrative voice. The tone of
the last sentence assures us that the light which the blind
bard has gained is better than the light he has lost because
it is stronger, steadier, truer, because it illumines the mind
with immortal vision. Yet the tone of the preceding sentence
reminds us that this inner light is not gained without painful
sacrifice, and that sacrifice is the loss of the sweetness and
simplicity of nature's rotating light, the loveliness of the rose
which bloomed perpetually and without thorns in the true
pastoral world of Eden. The speaker approves the sacrifice,
as Eve is reconciled to her banishment, because the light
which is gained illumines his prophetic song with the beauty
of unwavering truth, but like Eve he mourns the loss, be-
cause the light which is lost had its own beauty and value,
and he grieves that what is gained must be at the cost of so
much pain and waste.

The voice which we hear in the epic introductions to Books
I and III explicitly defines itself through the metaphors of
the bird and especially of the blind bard, metaphors sus-
tained and elaborated in the epic introductions to later books.
The invocation which opens Book VII serves again as a
transition from one world to another, and as a reminder
that although the previous episode and the narration which
is immediately to follow are told by the angel Raphael, his
words are reported to us by the narrator whose vision in-
cludes and communicates the angel's. Again the narrator
insists on his double relation to his readers and his song. As
bird he can "soare,/ Above the flight of *Pegasean* wing"
(VII, 3–4); yet if he is to achieve these heights safely, his

ascent must be "led" and his descent "guided" lest like Bellerophon he "fall" to earth "Erroneous, there to wander and forlorne" (VII, 20). As blind bard he dwells in "darkness" and "solitude" and yet the Muse illumines his mind with a light impervious alike to "Nightly" obscurity or the dawn which "Purples the East" (VII, 30). The same metaphors in the opening of Book IX support simultaneously the speaker's proud claim to a "higher Argument" than those of earlier epic poets and his prayer for inspiration to recite the tragic Fall of man, in which his own destiny was included. This is the voice which we hear throughout the narrative, descriptive, and discursive passages in *Paradise Lost*, the voice which interprets for us the actions and speeches of the characters. It is the epic introductions that create and define the narrator and establish the complex tone which characterizes his voice throughout the epic.

This complexity of tone depends upon the fact that both narrator and reader are involved in the epic argument, that we are made to interpret our own lost innocence by the light of our own experience in the fallen world. In the introduction to Book III, for example, or in Eve's lament for her banishment or in the descriptions of the Garden of Eden, our nostalgic feelings about the lost light of innocence are evoked not only by the lovely simplicity of the lines, but also by their references to the tradition of pastoral poetry. That tradition, although it celebrates the world of innocence which we and the speaker have lost, belongs itself to the fallen world. The tradition of pastoral poetry is the tradition of Hesperian fables, feigned by mortal imaginations, but because of the Fall, the narrator and the reader can interpret Eden only through these fables, unless their minds are illumined by the inner light.

Throughout the poem not only our longing for Eden and our sense of poignant loss, but still other attitudes and quite different emotions are evoked in us by the speaker's references to the poetry of the fallen world. In another passage from the introduction to Book III, for example, the narrator associates himself with poets and prophets of ancient renown:

> Blind *Thamyris* and blind *Mæonides*,
> And *Tiresias* and *Phineus* Prophets old.   (III, 35–36)

It is significant that he lists Greek rather than Biblical names here, and it is significant that he describes his dedication to poetry not only by the Old Testament reference to the waters of Sion, but also in pagan imagery:

> Yet not the more
> Cease I to wander where the Muses haunt
> Cleer Spring, or shadie Grove, or Sunnie Hill,
> Smit with the love of sacred song . . .   (III, 26–29)

This seems at first a curious way to describe the discipline and sacrifice demanded of a prophetic poet.[6] The speaker pictures himself as a lover "Smit" with passion and longing for the object of his desire. Yet he is also the blind bard, set apart from the "chearful waies of men" (III, 46), almost god-like in the special powers granted by his affliction. Here the verb "wander" does not suggest what it means in Eve's lament for her banishment, the sense of being bereft and aimless, lost without direction or guide. Here "wander" suggests the meaning it has in a passage later in the poem in which Raphael describes the divine creation of the true pastoral world:

> . . . Earth now
> Seemd like to Heav'n, a seat where Gods might dwell,
> Or wander with delight, and love to haunt
> Her sacred shades . . .   (VII, 328–331)

Both here and in Book III, the verb "wander" suggests freedom and a rich variety of choices, the sense of leisure to experience abundance and the sense of power to discriminate among its enjoyments. The same notion of a variety of possible choices is suggested in the lines from Book III by the contrasts of "shadie Grove" or "Sunnie Hill," contrasts which a blind man could feel as welcome coolness or warmth. This appeal to the senses, this feeling of freedom and variety of choice is evoked in these lines by the references to pagan poetry. Yet pagan poetry belongs to the world in which the fallen reader and the blind speaker now move, not the world of innocence, the pastoral world once true, which we lost when Adam and Eve were banished from Eden. Here, and throughout *Paradise Lost*, the allusions to the fables feigned by pagan poets evoke a sense of all the wealth of knowledge and feeling which has entered the world since Adam's Fall. By his disobedience we lost our original simplicity and innocence, but we gained a multiplicity of choices; we gained the beauty, the poignancy, and the variety of mortal experience.

The tone which is controlled in part by these literary figures and allusions, the tone which characterizes the narrative voice throughout *Paradise Lost*, derives its complexity from paradox, and this paradox is expressed in the double nature of the blind bard. Just as the narrator has been granted a truer vision in his blindness, and *because* he is blind, so Adam and Eve are granted what the Angel calls "A Paradise within thee, happier farr" (XII, 587) only *after* they have lost their first Paradise. So the reader can experience the abundance and variety of the fallen world — the source of image and allusion which gives the poem its richness and its scope — only after he has lost the true pastoral world, the innocence and simplicity of Eden. The tone implies that for the blind bard, for Adam and Eve, and for the reader, the world that is gained is in some sense more precious than what is lost, yet this implication is preserved from complacency by the awareness in the narrative voice of the beauty of Eden, of the terrible reality of the pain and loss, and also of the splendid precariousness of the freedom and variety of the fallen world.

This paradox, which is presented in the opening lines of the epic (what we lost by Adam's Fall is restored by "one *greater* Man"), is sustained by the narrative voice throughout the poem. Yet despite our continuous sense of the speaker's complex tone, it is only at the end of the poem, only after we have *experienced* the events of the narrative which is a re-enactment of our own spiritual history, that we can fully understand the paradox which the speaker expresses from the beginning.

In Books XI and XII Adam is granted a vision of the future, which is the history of our fallen world. At first the vision seems only to increase his sense of horror and guilt, for he sees that his sin lets loose in the world an endless variety of diseases, vices, idolatries, and crimes which are paraded before his eyes. Yet when he sees as the fulfillment of history the redemption offered by Christ for man's sins (the redemption predicted to the reader in the first epic introduction and explained in the Council in Heaven of Book III), and sees the final restoration of Paradise, his lament turns to joy and wonder:

> O goodness infinite, goodness immense!
> That all this good of evil shall produce,
> And evil turn to good; more wonderful
> Then that which by creation first brought forth
> Light out of darkness! full of doubt I stand,
> Whether I should repent me now of sin
> By mee done and occasiond, or rejoyce
> Much more, that much more good thereof shall spring,
> To God more glory, more good will to Men
> From God, and over wrauth grace shall abound.
>
> (XII, 469–478)

Adam has here apprehended as a theological truth the paradox that Eve has come to understand intuitively when she accepts her banishment from Paradise because she recognizes the true Eden within the soul. Just as without the Fall there would have been no occasion to demonstrate divine love in the redemption, so without the knowledge of evil that sin brought to Adam and Eve, they would never have learned the nature of good. The theological paradox of *felix culpa* which Adam has apprehended leads him to understand its ethical counterpart.[7] His experience of sin and his vision of its consequences enable him to recognize the true nature of heroism:

> Greatly instructed I shall hence depart,
> Greatly in peace of thought, and have my fill
> Of knowledge, what this vessel can containe;
> Beyond which was my folly to aspire.
> Henceforth I learne, that to obey is best,
> And love with feare the onely God, to walk
> As in his presence, ever to observe
> His providence, and on him sole depend,
> Merciful over all his works, with good
> Still overcoming evil, and by small
> Accomplishing great things, by things deemd weak
> Subverting worldly strong, and worldly wise
> By simply meek; that suffering for Truths sake
> Is fortitude to highest victorie,
> And to the faithful Death the Gate of Life . . .   (XII, 557–571)

The ethical paradox which this speech expresses, and its theological counterpart in Adam's earlier speech, provide the logic for Milton's justification of the "wayes of God to men."

But *Paradise Lost* is neither an ethical nor a theological treatise; nor is it a dramatic work in which any verbal meanings must necessarily be presented in speeches by characters. It is an epic poem and its chief means of making us *feel* the paradox is through the tone of the narrative voice. The speaker, whose double nature is revealed most fully by the metaphor of the blind bard, has from the beginning shared "our woe" at the same time that he has prophesied to us, and his prophetic song declares the great paradox that man's tragic Fall brings his glorious redemption. This is the voice which speaks the closing lines of the poem and this the paradox which controls the tone of these lines:

> Som natural tears they drop'd, but wip'd them soon;
> The World was all before them, where to choose
> Thir place of rest, and Providence thir guide:
> They hand in hand with wandring steps and slow,
> Through *Eden* took thir solitarie way,   (XII, 645–649)

The speaker here is the blind bard — himself banished from Eden to a dark and painful world yet guided by celestial light through its abundance and variety. Here the word "wandring" suggests again the sense of aimlessness and bewilderment that her banishment meant to Eve when she feared to "wander down" into the world of chance and change. Yet it also suggests the freedom and variety that the verb "wander" earlier meant to the speaker, cut off from the light of pastoral nature yet able to "wander" in the abundant world of poetry. This second meaning is reinforced in these lines by the accented word "all," suggesting again abundance and variety, and the word "choose," endowing man with the power to act and to discriminate.

This mingling of attitudes pervades the closing passage. Adam and Eve weep, and yet "soon" find comfort and resolution. They are "solitarie" — smaller, frail, and forlorn since the Fall — and indeed they are the only people in the whole unknown world; yet they are "hand in hand" again as before the Fall, with a oneness which in their affliction gains new dimensions of solace and responsibility. They must leave the simplicity and loveliness of their home in Eden for a strange world which seems to them wild and dark, and yet they have a goal which is "rest," and a "guide," which is the celestial light within them. We feel their loss of simplicity and innocence, and we never forget the greatness of that loss, yet we also feel their growth in self-knowledge and experience. We feel that they have lost the true pastoral world of Eden and entered the true heroic world of perilous yet glorious choice.

Our feelings are controlled here by the tone of the narrative voice, the mingling of attitudes which has characterized that tone from the opening of the epic. In its authority and in its sympathy the speaker's voice agrees with the divine injunction that Michael send Adam and Eve from the Garden "though sorrowing, yet in peace" (XI, 117). In its muted though hopeful accents this passage also echoes Michael's final injunction to fallen Adam:

> . . . go, waken *Eve*;
> Her also I with gentle Dreams have calm'd
> Portending good, and all her spirits compos'd
> To meek submission: thou at season fit
> Let her with thee partake what thou hast heard,
> Chiefly what may concern her Faith to know,
> The great deliverance by her Seed to come
> (For by the Womans Seed) on all Mankind.
> That ye may live, which will be many dayes,
> Both in one Faith unanimous though sad,
> With cause for evils past, yet much more cheer'd
> With meditation on the happie end.   (XII, 594–605)

Yet these last lines of the epic have a special quality. Almost as explicitly as the closing lines of *Lycidas*, they seem to reflect a change in the angle of vision. The speaker seems now at a greater distance from his subject. The figures seem to recede and grow smaller until we view them through his eyes as if framed in perspective. Like the speaker in *Lycidas*, the blind bard has assimilated the events of his own "great Argument," made them part of his personal experience and the reader's, that we may contemplate them now with "calm of mind all passion spent." The story of the Fall of Adam and Eve, by being re-enacted in his epic, has become one with his own private loss, and their hopeful restoration part of the pattern of his own recovery. All the cycles in the poem of descent and reascent, loss and restoration, departure and return are fully and finally harmonized for the reader and for the narrator in the tone of the closing lines, which conclude the song of the bird and the vision of the blind bard.

II · POINT OF VIEW AND COMMENT

The "World/ Of woe and sorrow" (VIII, 332–333), the world of storms and shadows, of change and loss, of variety and abundance, to which Adam and Eve are banished at the end of the poem, is the world in which the narrator and the reader of *Paradise Lost* now live. The tone of the speaker is controlled by his personal experience of this mortal world and his inspired vision of its contrast with the true pastoral world of Eden before the Fall and of the Paradise to come. The response of the reader to that tone is controlled by his awareness that he can *only* share the narrator's vision by contrasting the world that is lost with the only world he has ever known, the world that is gained by Adam and Eve through the paradox of the fortunate Fall.

The role of the narrator as interpreter to the fallen reader of the unfallen world, the world "invisible to mortal sight," determines the distinctive style of *Paradise Lost*. Truths which, according to Milton's outline in the Cambridge manuscript, were to be bodied forth in the allegorical "shapes" or "mask" of *Adam unparadiz'd*, are expressed in the epic poem by the narrator's elaborately sustained pattern of contrasts between the "invisible" world and our own. The bird's song, the blind bard's vision are of these contrasts and the style created for the narrative voice is designed to express these contrasts. The bird transcends the earth in his circular flight and the blind bard turns inward for heavenly illumination, while the reader remains in the mortal world, which is always the ground from which he looks back at the world which he lost in Adam's Fall. We know that we are continually meant to view the events of the poem from this lower world of chance and change because from the first lines the narrative voice repeatedly reminds us of our experience in this world. The reminders are made explicitly, in direct comments by the narrative voice, and implicitly, in many and varied devices which characterize Milton's style in *Paradise Lost*.

The epic introductions to Books I, III, VII, and IX are essential to the pattern of Milton's epic because, as we have seen, they create an identity for the narrative voice, and establish relations between the narrator and his characters and readers. This narrator, pictured as bird and especially as blind bard, is present without exception throughout the poem. Sometimes he directly addresses the Muse, or the characters, or the reader as mankind. Sometimes he narrates, describes, or explains, assuming mankind as his audience without directly identifying us. In other scenes he is himself the immediate audience or witness, endowed by his celestial patroness with a vision of Hell or Heaven or Eden, of events which occurred before the creation of the world and time, or of happenings to come when the world and time shall be no more. Nothing takes place in the poem which is not first spoken, or heard and retold by the narrative voice. Mood and meaning are consequently controlled by his tone,

and unless the reader remains aware of the distinctive role
of the narrative voice, he is liable to misinterpret mood and
meaning from his own position in the fallen world. To keep
the narrator in the center of his epic, Milton therefore de-
vised a large number of stylistic devices which give the lan-
guage of *Paradise Lost* its unique character.

The most simple of these devices is the speaker's practice
of explicitly distinguishing his own situation in space and
time from the experience of the readers of his poem or its
characters.[1] This device is particularly useful in the intro-
duction of a new scene, which is almost inevitably in the
poem the entrance into another world. The action of the
epic begins in Hell, which existed before the creation of the
world, or time, or men, and which in the theology of the
poem provided the reason for the creation of that world
and of man. The narrative voice must therefore interpret his
vision of Hell to us, who know only our own world, and it
is essential to Milton's design that we recognize the speaker's
role. The description of Hell begins then with a reminder:

> Nine times the Space that measures Day and Night
> To mortal men, he with his horrid crew
> Lay vanquisht, rowling in the fiery Gulfe
> Confounded though immortal . . .   (I, 50–53)

From the opening invocation of the epic, we, its audience,
have been prepared to include ourselves among "men." We
therefore recognize this elaborate way of phrasing "a long
time" or "as long as nine whole days" to be more than a
means of giving epic dignity to the style. It is a reminder
that we, the readers, have lost the unfallen ways of knowing,

that we are condemned to understand only in the dimension of time what the blind bard can conceive by other categories, by "Space" or some nontemporal scheme analogous to the unity of divine vision which encompasses all things simultaneously. Our identification not only as "men" but as "mortal" further reminds us that we are both limited and fallen, corrupted by the "mortal tast" which was the consequence of Satan's Fall. The sign of our mortality is that we must measure all experience by the passing of time, the diurnal course which to us means change and loss. We are meant to remember that the events of the poem have already occurred, to us and to the poet, and that it is because of what happens in the poem, because we and all men were corrupted by the Fall, that we stand in need of a guide to correct our reading of it. The narrative voice is our guide.

When the narrator reminds us of his complex relation to us, he usually at the same time places us in relation to his story and its characters. The description of Satan's host, for example, begins:

. . . For never since created man,
Met such imbodied force . . .   (I, 573–574)

Here it is not our "mortal" condition, but our "created" nature which we remember. We are God's creatures, like Satan, and our creation is as much a result of his fall as is our mortality; both are contained by God's will. In the beginning of the catalogue of devils we are told:

Nor had they yet among the Sons of *Eve*
Got them new Names . . .   (I, 364–365)

We are the "Sons of *Eve*." We are looking *back* with the

speaker on our own history, to the time when we gave the devils the names of false gods, and the narrator is interpreting for us that history before time which as "Sons of *Eve*" we cannot see. We are also looking *forward* to our own history, for to be "Sons of *Eve*" is to be redeemed as well as fallen, and the inspired speaker is reminding us of events which he can foresee and which we will share with him in the fullness of time.

With equal explicitness the narrator distinguishes his situation and therefore his vision from the situation and point of view of his characters. The first description of Hell, which contrasts the narrator's vision with the understanding of "mortal men," also sets him apart from Satan:

> At once as far as Angels kenn he views
> The dismal Situation waste and wilde . . . (I, 59–60)

"Angels kenn" is by implication more extensive than that of unaided "men," since without help Satan can survey Hell, but more limited than the narrator's, whose Muse is omniscient:

> . . . for Heav'n hides nothing from thy view
> Nor the deep Tract of Hell . . . (I, 27–28)

Unlike Satan, the speaker knows not only what is past, but what will be "Long after known in *Palestine*" (I, 80), the future outcome of the events in which Satan is involved, by which he is bound. To give one final illustration, the speaker describes the vision of the angels descending to banish man to the fallen world as "A glorious Apparition, had not doubt/ And carnal fear that day dimm'd *Adams* eye" (XI,

POINT OF VIEW [49

211–212). The contrast between the narrator's view and Adam's asserts that the speaker was in some sense present at the scene to see and judge for himself, that his sight and judgment are truer than our fallen vision or Adam's and are therefore the measure of meaning in the epic.

The voice which throughout the poem so often by a phrase distinguishes itself from reader and characters at times speaks out directly, even at length, to comment upon the action, to extend it into the past or future, or to interpret the motives of characters. These passages of "author-comment" have been isolated by critics as if they were detachable — didactic, non-dramatic, undemonstrated statements in a work which otherwise convincingly acts out its meanings in the manner of dramatic literature. A further assumption commonly associated with this attitude is that these comments are made personally by Milton, at moments when his private enthusiasms moved him to speak, as in the hymn to wedded love, or at other times when he felt the dramatic life of his poem might of its own accord dim his intention to justify God's ways, or threaten the rightness of his theological propositions.[2] These critical notions involve a number of misconceptions which must be examined if we are to see the way the narrative voice in Milton's epic controls its mood and meaning.

It is, as we have seen, misleading to call the speaker in *Paradise Lost* "Milton." In any narrative the author must find some sort of voice in which to speak; yet this voice, however much it may echo his private manner of talking, can never be equated with his total personality. Wordsworth in *The Prelude* invents a voice which he identifies as himself and he endows that speaker with a biography and attitudes and feelings selected from his own experience; yet if we call that voice "Wordsworth," we must remind ourselves that it is a sustained invention, the poet's conscious artistic creation. To call the narrator of *Paradise Lost* "Milton" is to violate his intention even more drastically. For it is part of Wordsworth's artistry to suggest the qualities of "speech," to deny art, to be "natural" rather than literary. The opening lines of *The Prelude* echo Milton's epic in part in order to point out Wordsworth's avoidance of its "poetical" qualities, its formality, its literary conventions. Milton's intention, on the other hand, is to exploit literary tradition, to intensify formality, to remind the reader continually of the elaborateness of his artistry. His poem is not talk but "song," not autobiography but inspired "vision." His narrator is not "himself" but a bird, or a bard who shares prophetic powers with Moses and Isaiah and Tiresias, who shares blindness with Milton himself, but also with Homer, with Samson, with the man cured by Jesus in the Gospel of John. To be sure, Milton's selection of images to portray the narrative voice must have been influenced by his own experience, and just as surely his private enthusiasms are often expressed by the speaker in the epic. But those images create an objectified voice with a distinct identity, tone, and manner, and the attitudes which the voice expresses are in keeping with that identity.

The other misconceptions involved in much critical discussion of the didactic comments in the epic are that these are the only occasions when we are made aware of a narrator and that his intention is to check the drift of the poem's dramatic life. Yet the speaker who utters the hymn to wedded love, the sermon on riches in Hell, the lecture against hypocrisy, the criticisms of corrupt clergy — these "preachier" passages in the epic — is the same speaker who describes Hell and Eden, who witnesses the council in Heaven, hears the love speeches of Adam and Eve, retells the fables of mortal poets. The direct addresses by this voice are not nervous attempts to correct the dramatic direction of the poem. They are reminders of the speaker's identity, that the reader may never lose his awareness of that distinctive voice in its unique situation. The explicit comments by the narrative voice are part of the total pattern, are essential to the expression of the speaker's vision, which directs the reader's interpretation by controlling the mood and meaning of every scene in the poem.

The description of Satan's entrance into Eden, again our introduction to a new and unknown world, provides a number of illustrations of how our interpretation is controlled by the narrator through direct comments working organically with all the other devices of narration.

We see the earthly Paradise for the first time on the occasion of Satan's entrance into it, but we do not see it as he does. The assertion often repeated by critics that we see Eden through Satan's eyes illustrates again the dangers of ignoring Milton's special narrator. These critics have, I believe, recognized in the tone that the observer of Eden is fallen, but have identified that tone with the character rather than with the speaker, whose presence they tend to discount or forget.[3] We are told what sights confront Satan, but those sights are described for us in the language of the narrator, not the language of the fallen Archangel, so that our interpretation of the scene we are made to imagine is the speaker's. His interpretation depends in part upon his knowledge that Satan did in fact enter the Garden, but he sees it independently of Satan's point of view and describes it so that we will feel what Satan cannot feel. For example, as Satan stands outside the Garden looking up at the trees which encircle and guard its wall, we are told that this wall "to our general Sire gave prospect large/ Into his neather Empire neighbouring round" (IV, 144–145). We are therefore taken into the scene while Satan is still excluded from it. We are included in its physical bounds and in its moral history; Adam is the "general Sire" of reader and narrator but not of Satan. The Garden can therefore never mean to Satan what it means to us because it was never his to lose. Next the speaker places us at a geographical distance from the character and his setting by showing us the outlines of the mountain Satan wishes to climb (IV, 172). This is not the way the hill looks to Satan "Now" trying to ascend it but how it is envisioned by the narrator. Then we are given an account of the undergrowth obstructing Satan's path:

> . . . so thick entwin'd,
> As one continu'd brake, the undergrowth
> Of shrubs and tangling bushes had perplext
> All path of Man and Beast that past that way . . .
>
> (IV, 174–177)

This is not the baffled report of the character himself, but an explanation in the voice of one who knows the nature of the obstacle and its history, knows that already on other occasions the tangled growths "had perplext" man and animals.

These distinctions in point of view are expressed in part by complicated alternations of tense. To Satan the setting is physically present; the events are happening to him in the present time, or belong to his immediate past or future. To the reader Eden and all the events of the story are long past (our final redemption is not a part of the action of the poem but the subject of a prediction made in the past about our future). The speaker as fallen man shares our previous history, but as a blind bard inspired with supernatural vision, he miraculously experiences the events and places of prehistory in the present and miraculously sees into the future. His manipulations of tenses therefore transcend our experiences of time, logic, grammar. Satan's entrance into Eden begins, "So on he fares" (IV, 131); we watch as he "comes" in the present "Now nearer" (IV, 133) (Milton's equivalent in English for the Latin "historical present"); but then we are told of the obstacle which "deni'd" him access to the Garden (IV, 137), and the description continues in the past tense until the "now purer aire/ Meets his approach" (IV, 153–154). When later in the scene Satan as cormorant descends from his perch in the Tree of Life, his actions are described first in the present tense. He "alights" (IV, 396), but that verb is modified by the previous word "Then." Next we are told as if it were past action how he assumed whatever disguises "servd" his ends (IV, 398), but this action is modified by repetitions of "now." In this first description of Eden and throughout the poem, by such shifts in tense we are introduced as to a scene in a dramatic work without being allowed to forget the voice which interprets to us all the meanings of the scene by its contrast with our own present.

Once we are told that "th' arch-fellon" has lawlessly entered the Garden (and the use of the epithet reminds us again of the epic poet's presence), we are then given two similes which elaborate that action, as the preceding pair of similes had elaborated the sense impressions created by the scene:

> As when a prowling Wolfe,
> Whom hunger drives to seek new haunt for prey,
> Watching where Shepherds pen thir Flocks at eeve
> In hurdl'd Cotes amid the field secure,
> Leaps o're the fence with ease into the Fould:
> Or as a Thief bent to unhoord the cash
> Of some rich Burgher, whose substantial dores,
> Cross-barrd and bolted fast, fear no assault,
> In at the window climbes, or o're the tiles;
> So clomb this first grand Thief into Gods Fould . . .
>
> (IV, 183–192)

As we shall see later in detail, similes are one of the most important marks of the speaker's style. Here it is enough to recognize their self-consciousness. The speaker seems to be calling attention to his deliberate artistry by using a conventional rhetorical device. The similes do tell us more about Satan, or more accurately, give us ways of feeling for Satan and his victims. He is like a wolf or a thief or a bad priest — dangerous, malevolent, greedy, furtive; man is like an innocent lamb or a guarded but all the more naive and vulnerable citizen. But the extended similes also make us more aware of the narrator. They remind us that he is a poet

familiar with the literary conventions of epic and a man
familiar with a life infinitely remote from the vision he is
presenting. He knows the fallen world of innocence de-
stroyed, of petty viciousness, of corruption even in God's
Church. Yet his familiarity with mortal verse and his ex-
perience of mortal vice do not destroy his understanding of
the archetypal world. He can penetrate Satan's disguise (the
ambiguity of "Sat like a Cormorant" in line 196 suggests
either that Satan has assumed the form of the bird or that
the narrator is describing him by comparing him to a shape
more familiar to the reader). He knows what Satan is think-
ing, knows what Satan does not know (IV, 197–198). Be-
cause he can penetrate beyond our perception of surfaces,
this speaker can interpret for us the moral meaning of the
action:

> So little knows
> Any, but God alone, to value right
> The good before him, but perverts best things
> To worst abuse, or to thir meanest use. (IV, 201–204)

This is not "Milton" suddenly intervening between Satan's
point of view and the reader in order to speak out on his
favorite theme, misused freedom. This is the same narrator
who has described the hill, the undergrowth, and Satan's
actions, who has uncovered his dissembling and told us his
hidden schemes. It is the same narrator who will describe
to us what "To all delight of human sense" (IV, 206) — his,
our own, and Adam's — is exposed but not to Satan's, who
"Saw undelighted all delight" (IV, 286). It is the same voice
who will predict "Our Death" (IV, 221) in which, with that
phrase, he acknowledges and laments his share.

These didactic comments remind us of the narrator's presence and his special vision in order that we may accept his moral interpretation of the story. They are intended to remind us that what we see and feel differs from Satan's experience of the Garden as it will differ from unfallen Adam's. They are not *opposed* to the action of the poem, but are part of the total pattern of that action, not checks upon our immediate responses to drama, but a means of expressing the speaker's double point of view, his fallen knowledge and his inspired vision. To detach the moral comments as the sole expressions of the narrator's attitude is to oversimplify and flatten it, to make the speaker an unauthorized judge who lectures us like a prig just when we are most involved in the story.

The scene of Adam's Fall illustrates most fully the way direct moral comment works with other stylistic devices to express the whole response of the speaker to his argument.[4] Adam's "mortal tast" is accompanied by a didactic statement:

> . . . he scrupl'd not to eat
> Against his better knowledge, not deceav'd,
> But fondly overcome with Femal charm.   (IX, 997–999)

If this were all that the narrative voice had to say about the Fall of man, we would reject the authority of that voice. If we assume these lines to be spoken as if by a witness silent until now, who has therefore clearly not shared our response to the preceding scene, they seem to us altogether insufficient for the action. Taken by themselves as the sole response of which the speaker is capable, these lines would characterize him as unfeeling and inhumane, complacent

because willfully blind to the complexities of human experi-
ence. For the scene of Adam's Fall has evoked our sympathy,
our sorrow, our fear, and even our admiration, not a simple
condemnation. This comment upon Adam's action is, how-
ever, only part of the speaker's total response, an organic
and harmonious part. All the speeches which have moved
us have been reported to us by the narrative voice whose de-
scription and narration are one whole with his moralizing.
He, as well as the reader, sympathizes with man's plight,
acknowledges his greatness, shares and laments his loss. It
is in fact his complexity of response which evokes our own.

The scene of Adam's Fall begins immediately after Eve's
decision to offer Adam the fruit that she thinks may kill
him. The contrast between her knowing self-interest and his
still innocent ignorance and generosity is created by the
voice of the narrator:

> *Adam* the while
> Waiting desirous her return, had wove
> Of choicest Flours a Garland to adorne
> Her Tresses, and her rural labours crown
> As Reapers oft are wont thir Harvest Queen.   (IX, 838–842)

Here the narrative voice expresses in its tone affectionate
approval of Adam's pretty action. The diction is very simple
and the repetition of "her," emphasized by alliteration of
er sounds, is contrasted with the reiterated "I" of Eve's
speech. The one-line simile evokes by the simplest allusion
the pastoral world to which Adam still belongs but which
to Eve is lost forever and to us is known only in fables. He
has our sympathy because he is like the simple reaper, as
natural and dignified and loving as his unpretentious gift,

which we know will never again please Eve, now aspiring above her station as "Harvest Queen," now sophisticated and artificial in her taste, now jaded by the serpent's courtly "overpraising" (IX, 615). Contrasts in the speaker's style in the next passage sustain our feelings for Adam:

> Great joy he promis'd to his thoughts, and new
> Solace in her return, so long delay'd;
> Yet oft his heart, divine of something ill,
> Misgave him; hee the faultring measure felt;
> And forth to meet her went, the way she took
> That Morn when first they parted; by the Tree
> Of Knowledge he must pass, there he her met,
> Scarse from the Tree returning; in her hand
> A bough of fairest fruit that downie smil'd,
> New gatherd, and ambrosial smell diffus'd.   (IX, 843–852)

Adam is pictured here as the simple pastoral man, so fully in harmony with nature that he can feel its "faultring measure," yet vulnerable in his innocence, and in his love a prey to the temptations of a woman who will speak to him in the language of a more subtle, vicious world. His actions are described in metrically regular lines composed of monosyllables and ending with accented verbs, while Eve's smiling deviousness is suggested by words and lines having feminine endings, irregular in meter but mellifluous with profuse alliteration.

The voice which controls our response in this narrative passage is the voice of the same speaker who reports to us the speeches of the characters. We are reminded of his presence as audience and witness by the interpretive phrases with which he introduces the speeches, phrases which suggest that he knows already what words will be spoken, and can penetrate their meanings. Eve's "excuse" or "Apologie" is introduced by such a phrase: "Which with bland words at will she thus addrest" (IX, 855). The adjective "bland" warns us that Eve's former sweetness has turned to soothing suavity spoken "at will," which suggests that the smoothness of her words is calculated, that calculated speech now comes easily to her, and that it is no longer guided by her reason. This warning, given us in advance by the narrator, proves to be just. Eve's words *are* bland, calculated, willful. She glosses over, she exaggerates, she even tells lies. Next the narrator, having rightly predicted how her words would sound to us, describes for us how Adam responds to them:

> On th' other side, *Adam*, soon as he heard
> The fatal Trespass don by *Eve*, amaz'd,
> Astonied stood and Blank, while horror chill
> Ran through his veins, and all his joynts relax'd;
> From his slack hand the Garland wreath'd for *Eve*
> Down drop'd, and all the faded Roses shed:
> Speechless he stood and pale, till thus at length
> First to himself he inward silence broke.   (IX, 888–895)

No "bland words" can deceive still unfallen Adam. He recognizes her action as a "Trespass" and a "fatal" one. His response is at once both physical and moral, like the response of Nature herself (IX, 782–784). It is as if he felt already the chill touch of death, like the faded roses in Eve's intended crown. His dilemma is expressed in these lines — his love, his loss, his inevitable death — and the tone of the narrative voice controls our feeling for his dilemma. Our fear, evoked in part by the ugly diction, harsh consonants, and deep *o* sounds of the preceding lines, is mixed with the pity and nostalgia we feel at the allusion to the blossoms of the lost pastoral world. With Adam and with the speaker, we feel the beauty of the love which the garland symbolizes and we grieve for the fading of that beauty, at the same time that we feel the horror of the choice which Adam does not hesitate to make. For in the very act of choosing Eve he is destined to lose her, because they and we will be doomed to mortality; and Adam knows this. His speech is moving, passionate, romantic, but it is never deceived. He knows that Eve is like the garland "Defac't, deflourd, and now to Death devote" (IX, 901). He knows that they are "ruind" (IX, 906) and resigns himself to that ruin. His choice is to die *with* Eve, not *for* her, and already his passion is a kind of beautiful self-concern. Because his fear is for his own loneliness without her, not for her plight, the very union which he claims indissoluble is severed by his self-concern, and "I" becomes the center of his consciousness as it became for Eve when she had eaten the forbidden fruit (IX, 795–833) and as it had been for Adam before the completion of himself in Eve's creation (VIII, 267–282). In these lines he is even speaking to himself, which no longer means speaking to Eve.

By the tone of the narrative voice in the lines addressed to the reader between Adam's first speech to himself and his words to Eve, we know that the speaker who is our guide is not inhumanely indifferent to Adam's tragedy:

> So having said, as one from sad dismay
> Recomforted, and after thoughts disturbd
> Submitting to what seemd remediless,
> Thus in calme mood his Words to *Eve* he turnd. (IX, 917–920)

These lines express sympathy rather than condemnation, but

the words "seemd remediless" suggest that more than this
simple response is appropriate to Adam's speech. Most obvi-
ously, these words mean that it seems to Adam that he must
resign himself to death because he cannot choose to live
without Eve. To the reader and the speaker, also, this seems
to be his irremediable plight, for we have been moved by the
familiar accents of passion and loneliness and fear, emotions
which seem to us inescapable in human experience. We recog-
nize and grieve for Adam's plight, which seems without
remedy to us in still another sense, because our experience
of the mortal world he is now to enter teaches us that Adam's
choice of Eve dooms him to lose her. Yet the verb "seem"
in the poem is almost always a warning against oversimpli-
fication. The narrative voice uses it to remind us that unlike
other epics, his cannot be interpreted by mortal imaginations
alone, that contrasted with our fallen knowledge is the in-
spired vision of the blind bard whose darkness is purged
by the inner light. What "seems" true to the fallen reader
and speaker and to Adam as he sins may not be divine truth.
The words "remediless" and "Recomforted" can then recall
the truth that Adam chooses to ignore, that there is a Rem-
edy and a Comforter for those who use their free will to
follow reason, love virtue, obey God. His willful choice to
share with Eve either "bliss or woe" (IX, 916) is really a
willful choice of "woe," a word consistently associated in
the poem with Hell. By choosing to follow Eve he is reject-
ing the possibility of "bliss," the state of angels in Heaven
and of unfallen man in his "blissful Paradise" (IV, 208) on
earth. The choice is not inevitable; it is his sin that he
chooses to think it is.

The warning, here gently hinted by the narrator, is justified by the speeches which he then reports. Adam's words to Eve sound less noble than his previous speech. Like Eve after the Fall, like the monster Sin herself, he generates sins which quickly multiply: despair (IX, 926), ambition (935–937), blasphemy (938–941), and finally the absurd pride to think as Satan does that the fame of the Creator should depend upon the fate of the creature (948–950). Like Satan he has chosen the "Lot" of the damned, and with Eve he will "undergoe like doom" (IX, 953). His final appeal to the "Bond of Nature" (IX, 956) is at once an excuse and a mistake. He is wrong to claim that his nature predetermines him, since we have already been shown the act of sin as a violation of nature, and wrong to insist that Eve cannot be "severd" from him since he himself had earlier predicted the danger of such an unnatural separation (IX, 252). Yet because he has ceased to reason he can no longer recognize false from true language. His last words before the Fall reverberate with irony which only the narrator and the reader can hear. When Adam says "to loose thee were to loose my self" (IX, 959), he means only that he cannot live without Eve. But to us, because we have an inspired interpreter, the words mean also that he has in fact lost Eve, for she will die, at the same time he has also lost himself, as Satan is lost, as he knew Eve to be "lost" (IX, 900), because he will die and because he is damned.

Eve's lies in the following speech justify even more loudly the narrator's warning that to fallen minds there is a discrepancy between what "seems" and what is. By lying, she is deliberately exploiting that discrepancy at the same time that she is its helpless victim. The oneness with Adam which she seeks is lost forever. The "happie trial" (IX, 975) in which she triumphs is a mockery (and as terrible a distortion of the heavenly trial of love in Book III as was Satan's hateful sacrifice in Book II), for, though she cannot see it, both the meaning of the word "love" and the capacity to feel it have already been transformed by the Fall.

These speeches prepare us to question Eve's concept of "enobl'd" love (IX, 992). Adam's speech to himself was beautiful, with the beauty of mortal poetry which celebrates human love and loss; but the narrative voice has warned us to question that poetry, and the warning is brilliantly justified in fallen Adam's first speech when he proves himself to be the ancestor of Paris,[5] who threw away honor for love and whose passion was fabled to have brought mankind a "world of woe":

> For never did thy Beautie since the day
> I saw thee first and wedded thee, adorn'd
> With all perfections, so enflame my sense
> With ardor to enjoy thee, fairer now
> Then ever, bountie of this vertuous Tree.   (IX, 1029–1033)

The metaphors of fire which are repeated here in the lines spoken by and about Adam tell us that already he shares Satan's "lot." The same "hot Hell" (IX, 467) burns within them both. Love has become lust and Eden is Hell.

The didactic comment which the narrative voice makes as Adam eats is not an isolated interruption by "Milton," intended to check our unqualified sympathy for the drama of Adam's Fall. It is a part of the total pattern of the speaker's feelings as he reports and interprets the Fall to fallen men. It is spoken by the voice of the same narrator who has been moved by Adam's love speech, yet who knows and cautions against the limits of that feeling, who finds that caution justified by the cheapening of Adam's language which comes with the degeneration of his emotions. Yet even at this moment of severest condemnation the speaker does not lose all his sympathy for Adam, "fondly overcome with Femal charm" (IX, 999). The word "fondly" means not only "foolishly" but "lovingly," and the word "charm" suggests that Eve's powers do exist, that about them too he is not deceived, that her beauty and "sweet Converse and Love" (IX, 909), almost like the magical enchantments of a Circe, have overcome him. Adam therefore deserves our condemnation as a willful sinner at the same time that he retains our sympathy as a helpless victim.

The narrator's lines immediately after this comment intensify the expression of his grief and sympathy for Adam:

> Earth trembl'd from her entrails, as again
> In pangs, and Nature gave a second groan,
> Skie lowr'd, and muttering Thunder, som sad drops
> Wept at compleating of the mortal Sin
> Original . . .   (IX, 1000–1004)

The speaker's response to the Fall is one with Nature's. The earth is torn by the horror of the act (as it was to be again when Christ died to redeem Adam's Fall), at the same time that the sky weeps with sorrow for man's suffering and death. Heaven itself expresses both anger and grief in the thunderbolts of wrath and the waters of mercy. This passage marks the climax of feelings evoked by the scene of Adam's Fall. These feelings are shared by the reader only because his interpretation of the scene has been controlled by the narrative voice, by the fusion of direct moral comment with the many other devices of language used to express the wholeness of the blind bard's vision, the harmony of the bird's song.

In this scene and throughout the poem didactic comment is expressed in a language of statement, in diction which largely avoids allusiveness, figurative concreteness, or the evocation of a multiplicity of conflicting feelings. This is one kind of language which characterizes the blind bard, now cut off from the changing light of nature, from the colors and surfaces of things and the varied ways of men. This is the language in which he prays for the inner light to "see and tell/ Of things invisible to mortal sight," and the very abstractness of these statements is one means of reminding us that the speaker's moral vision of his argument surpasses our fallen understanding by its steadiness, its wholeness, its purity.

Yet even in his role as moral interpreter, prophetic seer, he never ceases to admit that we share experiences and values with him. He recognizes the possibilities of error and confusion and vice which we meet daily and at the same time trusts our rationality and virtue. He assumes that we recognize and deplore with him the corruption of the clergy, that we too condemn hypocrisy, that we are also appalled by the "bought smile/ Of Harlots, loveless, joyless, unindeard,/ Casual fruition" (IV, 765–767). He is even capable of a comment which seems to me effective in its mild amusement and sympathy — "No fear lest Dinner coole"

(V, 396) — because it reminds us that he shares with us a world different in its homeliest details from the one which he is interpreting to us. The language of statement has the authority of the divine light which it reflects, but it never loses sympathy with the characters in the poem or loses faith in the capacity of the reader's mind to be illumined by the inner light, his feelings to be stirred by heavenly harmonies.

III · SIMILE AND CATALOGUE

Because of the narrator's double nature, because as fallen man he shares all our ways of knowing, the speaker does not always address us in a language of statement. His style is also characterized by another kind of language — allusive, detailed, evocative — a language which makes the invisible world known to us by its analogies with our mortal experience. This language draws on the variety and abundance of the world to which Adam and Eve are banished, the world of nature and history and art that we and the speaker as heirs of Adam share. It is in part the combination of these two kinds of language which characterizes Milton's narrative voice and gives the style of his epic its unique effects.

From our situation in the fallen world we look back as the narrator directs us to our own prehistory, but we are never meant to forget that it is lost to us and that we can only know it by contrasts. One of the chief means of evoking these contrasts is by the speaker's use of similes. Similes are used most simply in literature as a way of comparing. They are always presented as if to make some notion clear, as if to give illuminating information about one term of the comparison by likening it to something else which it somehow resembles. The clarity of the comparison depends in part on the degree of resemblance, and also in part upon the familiarity of the term to which the unknown is compared, and its concreteness.

The extended simile, traditionally associated with epic poetry, professes to have this simple function at the same time that its elaboration, its self-consciousness, and its conventionality usually deny that simplicity. The pointed way in which the known term of the comparison is elaborated far beyond its resemblance to the less-familiar term denies (at the same time that it professes) the use of similes for comparison. The effect of this assumed simplicity is to make the heroic simile seem a sophisticated rhetorical device, the polished fruit of literary experience, of training, and of taste. This sophistication was thought to be suited to epic because it added to the dignity of the style and to the impression of the heroic poet as a man of vast learning and lofty imagination, who could survey the whole world of experience in search of just and discriminating comparisons.

The extended simile was also thought to be suited to heroic poetry because of its inclusiveness. Without disturbing the desired unity of structure, epic similes could be used to add variety to the poem, to widen its range of reference and to ornament its poetic surface. In similes the poet could claim his relationship to a wealth of literary tradition, by their formal conventionality and by their allusions to other poems, to other literature, and to other learning.

Similes in *Paradise Lost* do add to the dignity of the style by their deliberate artistry, and they do give a sense of variety and weight by their vast and learned allusiveness. Milton exploited the traditional uses of the device and wished his readers to recognize this achievement. By echoing the form and often the content of classical similes, by referring to ancient myths in his own comparisons, he calls our attention to the tradition in which he claims to be writing. In *Paradise Lost*, however, the extended similes are used in very individual ways to suit the unique demands of his "great Argument" and its "answerable style." These extended similes, especially combined as they are with the didactic comments, are a means of characterizing the narrative voice, of enriching his tone, of insisting on his presence and enlarging his role as our interpreter and guide. The similes elaborate and sustain the pattern of contrasts between the world of "things invisible to mortal sight" and our fallen world which controls the mood and meaning of the poem.

The similes which we remember from *Paradise Lost*, those which seem to give the poetry its special texture, are all spoken by the narrative voice. They are a distinctive mark of his manner of speaking and of the ways in which his style expresses a vision different from that of his characters. This careful use of similes to distinguish the narrator's style from the speeches of his characters is one of Milton's most elaborate means of transforming the drama of Adam's Fall into a narrative poem whose meaning is expressed in the tone of the speaker.

Ancient and orthodox tradition guided Milton to create in *Paradise Lost* a God who speaks a language of statement. The conventional figures of poetry or rhetoric would have seemed blasphemously inappropriate to God, who needs no comparisons because He can survey all things "from his prospect high,/ Wherein past, present, future, he beholds" simultaneously (III, 77–78).[1] The same tradition and reverent sense of decorum inspired Milton to avoid similes in his description of Heaven, the incomparable realm of uncreated light. This is the only descriptive passage spoken directly by the narrative voice which does not employ extended similes.

Traditional theology also taught that there is a difference between angels' ways of knowing and man's. Raphael explains the difference to Adam by distinguishing their forms of reasoning:

> Discursive, or Intuitive; discourse
> Is oftest yours, the latter most is ours . . .   (V, 488–489)

It is not surprising, then, to find that the angelic narrators in *Paradise Lost* speak a different language from the speaker, who shares our human nature and our fallen condition. The episodes of Books V, VI, VII, and VIII which are narrated by the angel Raphael, as well as the future history told to Adam by Michael in Book XII, differ in style from the narrator's manner chiefly in their avoidance of extended similes.

The angel Raphael is an interpreter who, like the poem's speaker, undertakes "Sad task and hard" (V, 564) to unfold "what surmounts the reach/ Of human sense" (V, 571–572) by employing the illustrative device of comparison. He repeatedly announces his intention to "set forth/ Great things by small" (VI, 310–311), unknown by familiar (V, 571–574; VI, 893). This is his deliberate means of accommodating his immediate intuition to Adam's discursive ways of knowing. Yet although Raphael is an interpreter, like the narrator, he is neither a fallen human being nor an epic poet.

His comparisons therefore differ in kind and in function from those which characterize the narrative voice.

Raphael's similes reveal the nature of his vision and also of Adam's, for they are intended to help Adam's understanding and so must draw comparisons from within his experience. Of necessity they are therefore much simpler than the speaker's similes, because Adam has almost no experience. He has no past and until he has fallen, has in our sense virtually no future, since by the future we mean a change, something different from what is or has been. He has no other worlds, no times or places with which to compare his own, has only Eve, the animals, and the angels to contrast with himself. He can realize differences because he recognizes hierarchy, degrees of existence leading up to God, and he knows the book of the creatures, but that is the range of his unfallen experience.

The angel's comparisons are therefore drawn most often from the world of unfallen nature surrounding Adam in Eden. This nature is described in language associated for us with pastoral literature; yet for us pastoral is a sophisticated, artificial, conventional recreation of a language which for Adam and the angels was simple, natural, and immediate because it was a true description of the unfallen world. Typical is the pair of similes with which the angel describes Satan's host:

> Innumerable as the Starrs of Night,
> Or Starrs of Morning, Dew-drops, which the Sun
> Impearls on every leaf and every flouer.   (V, 745–747)

The objects of unfallen nature which provide Raphael's comparisons have this quality of pastoral innocence, even when they are used as in these lines to describe what is vicious or violent. Satan's countenance is alluring like the morning star (V, 708), his words are greeted with a murmur like the "sound of waters deep" (V, 872), his defeated armies resemble "timorous" flocks (VI, 857), the armies of God a formation of birds (VI, 73–74). To use as comparisons events in themselves suggesting danger or conflict, Raphael is driven to suppositions:

> . . . as if on Earth
> Winds under ground or waters forcing way
> Sidelong, had push't a Mountain from his seat
> Half sunk with all his Pines.   (VI, 195–198)

Adam must try to imagine storms and earthquakes, or again try to suppose:

> . . . If Natures concord broke,
> Among the Constellations warr were sprung,
> Two Planets rushing from aspect maligne
> Of fiercest opposition in mid Skie,
> Should combat, and thir jarring Sphears confound.
>   (VI, 311–315)

To describe the separation of land and sea, Raphael is even forced to draw on his own previous account of the armies embattled in Heaven to find a comparison familiar to Adam:

> . . . as Armies at the call
> Of Trumpet (for of Armies thou hast heard)
> Troop to thir Standard, so the watrie throng,
> Wave rowling after Wave, where way they found,
> If steep, with torrent rapture, if through Plaine,
> Soft-ebbing . . .   (VII, 295–300)

In search of some way to describe the march of armies, Raphael draws his comparison from one of the few unique experiences Adam has ever had:

> . . . as when the total kind
> Of birds in orderly array on wing
> Came summond over *Eden* to receive
> Thir names of thee . . .   (VI, 73–76)

The only comparison which Adam himself makes when he recounts to the angel the one story that he knows has the same pastoral qualities of freshness, simplicity, and sweetness that are typical of Raphael's similes: Eve's blushes are like the rosiness of dawn (VIII, 511).

If Raphael's intention in using these similes is simply to aid Adam's understanding, Milton's reasons for assigning pastoral images to the angel are more complex. By this selection of comparisons he emphasizes the character of the unfallen world, the purity of angelic vision, and the innocence of man's first condition. The familiar terms of the comparisons are all drawn from a nature as yet untroubled by change or violence or death. The stars, the dewdrops, the ocean's waters all represent a benevolent order and beauty surrounding man, the animals a due subordination to his kingship. The relative brevity and simplicity of these similes also express in form the directness of understanding, the unclouded and undistracted vision of unfallen reason.

Contrasted with these similes of the true pastoral world (and the contrast is altogether too consistent to be accidental) are the similes which characterize the style of the speaker.

The contrast expresses the differences between the angelic narrator and the blind bard, and between Raphael's audience, unfallen Adam, and Milton's readers, whom his narrator addresses as fallen mankind.

The most immediately obvious qualities of the similes spoken by the narrative voice in *Paradise Lost* are their richness, their elaborateness, and their variety. Their content is drawn from a number of different sources: from nature, from history both classical and Biblical, from philosophy, science or pseudo-science, folklore, farming, city life. Often they are literary, with a self-consciousness, a deliberate conventionality and artifice which contrast with the simply descriptive function of Raphael's true pastoral language. Their functions are varied: they provide information, condense past action, predict the future, control mood.[2] Yet they are all spoken by one voice, reflect the experience of one speaker. As a way of characterizing the epic narrator, the heroic similes in *Paradise Lost*, whatever their content or narrative function or structure, express over and over the same qualities of experience, attitude, vision — qualities which are the antithesis of those expressed in the similes spoken by the angel to unfallen Adam.

The similes of the narrator are more extended and elaborate than Raphael's, more often linked in long series. For example, Raphael in only three lines compares the vastness of Satan's armies to stars and dewdrops. The speaker, on the other hand, uses a negative comparison of fifteen lines in which he lists the armies of epic renown (I, 572–587), while earlier in the poem he describes the numbers of the fallen host in an eleven-line series of three different comparisons:

                . . . he stood and call'd
His Legions, Angel Forms, who lay intrans't
Thick as Autumnal Leaves that strow the Brooks
In *Vallombrosa*, where th' *Etrurian* shades
High overarch't imbowr; or scatterd sedge
Afloat, when with fierce Winds *Orion* arm'd
Hath vext the Red-Sea Coast, whose waves orethrew
Busiris and his *Memphian* Chivalrie,
While with perfidious hatred they pursu'd
The Sojourners of *Goshen*, who beheld
From the safe shore their floating Carkases
And broken Chariot Wheels, so thick bestrown
Abject and lost these lay, covering the Flood . . .

                                        (I, 300–312)

This series is typical of the speaker's similes. By the self-
conscious elaboration of the second term of the comparison
far beyond the original point of resemblance — vast num-
bers — and the artful linking of three connected legends,
the narrative voice seems to call attention to the rhetorical
figure itself, to its intricate form and heroic content. Such
a simile denies the simple function of elucidation. It delib-
erately reveals more about the imagination which conceives
it and the world from which its substance is drawn than
about the unknown term of the comparison. Of course the
implication is that Satan's host shares more than vastness
with the subjects of the legends, shares power, fierceness, a
sinister kind of glamor, but those qualities are first asserted
to belong to the speaker's world. They are the same qualities
conveyed in the comparison of Satan's armies to the armies
fabled by mortal poets, of Satan himself to the leviathan
or to a griffin or a comet, and in a great many of the other
similes spoken by the narrative voice.

This series of comparisons is representative, then, not only in its structure, but also in what its content suggests. There are an extraordinary number of names in this passage, names of particular places and figures of fable and history, again a common characteristic of the narrator's similes. In the comparison of Satan's army to those of epic fame, for example, fifteen such names are listed. In other similes his shield is likened to the moon viewed from "Fesole" or "Valdarno" (I, 289–290), his spear to a mast of "Norwegian" pine (I, 293). These names are of course evocative by their mere sounds and by their legendary or historical associations, which Milton expected his readers to know. Yet they also suggest something about the experience shared by the speaker and his readers. The special reference of the names, their insistence on differences, on individuality, on the detailed and the concrete, expresses the nature of the fallen world. Such names were not invented until after the Fall, as Michael explains to Adam (XII, 140), but they are the only way we have of talking about our world. The archetypes of prehistory are shattered; the Garden of Eden, where names were the names of genus — of "herb," "tree," "fruit," and "flour" — or of species designated according to their natures, has been transformed into a world which we can know only in fragments, which we experience in its details rather than its wholeness.

Combined with the insistence on names in the narrator's similes is a preoccupation with particular times of day or year. The armies are numberless as "Autumnal" leaves, or as bees in "spring time" (I, 769). Mammon's speech is greeted with a murmur like the sound of winds which "all night long" disturb the ocean waves (II, 286), while Beelzebub commands attention "still as Night/ Or Summers Noon-tide air" (II, 308–309). Sometimes an entire simile is devoted to changes of season or weather or time of day, like the one which describes the change of mood after Satan addresses Hell's host:

> As when from mountain tops the dusky clouds
> Ascending, while the North wind sleeps, o'respread
> Heavn's chearful face, the lowring Element
> Scowls ore the dark'nd lantskip Snow, or showre;
> If chance the radiant Sun with farewell sweet
> Extend his ev'ning beam, the fields revive,
> The birds thir notes renew, and bleating herds
> Attest thir joy, that hill and valley rings.   (II, 488–495)

More often the detail of time or season is irrelevant to the logic of the comparison, though evocative of a particular mood or sense impression. Satan is compared to a wolf "Watching where Shepherds pen thir Flocks at eeve" (IV, 185). Uriel is described flying "swift as a shooting Starr/ In *Autumn* thwarts the night" (IV, 556–557). The dwarfing of Satan's followers is described in a double comparison which by its allusions to particulars evokes the sense of wonder, remoteness, and mystery that so often characterizes the narrator's similes:

> . . . they but now who seemd
> In bigness to surpass Earths Giant Sons
> Now less then smallest Dwarfs, in narrow room
> Though numberless, like that Pigmean Race
> Beyond the *Indian* Mount, or Faerie Elves,
> Whose midnight Revels, by a Forrest side
> Or Fountain some belated Peasant sees,
> Or dreams he sees, while over head the Moon
> Sits Arbitress, and neerer to the Earth
> Wheels her pale course . . .   (I, 777–786)

The same evocative qualities are found in the last extended simile in the poem in which the narrator compares the descent of angels to the way

> . . . Ev'ning Mist
> Ris'n from a River o're the marish glides,
> And gathers ground fast at the Labourers heel
> Homeward returning.   (XII, 629–632)

Comparisons with the fables of mortal poets often include the apparently irrelevant mention of time or season. Adam, the speaker tells us:

> Smil'd with superior Love, as *Jupiter*
> On *Juno* smiles, when he impregns the Clouds
> That shed May Flowers . . .   (IV, 499–501)

Or the fables themselves concern changes of season or weather: "as when *Zephyrus* on *Flora* breathes" (V, 16). Proserpina's story is compared to Eve's not only because it tells of innocence threatened, but because it appeals to the narrator's concern with the seasons and their melancholy changes.

The attention to particular times of day or season or weather, like the insistence on the names of particular places and figures, reflects the quality of experience which the narrator and the reader share. As human beings we are always bound by time and space, and as fallen men we are ruled by change. We can never escape the seasons; our lives are controlled by the weather, light and darkness, all the cycles of nature. This is the special mark of mortal existence, distinguishing it from the world of prehistory. The devils in Hell experience no such existence, for they are fixed forever in a realm which knows no light, no spring, no hope of change. The changelessness of Hell is the negative of the eternity of Heaven, the realm of unwavering light, where grow the "Immortal Amarant" and the "Celestial Roses" that will "never fade" (III, 360). Unlike Hell or Heaven, Eden experiences the cycles of nature but to unfallen Adam and Eve they form a "Perpetual Circle" of perfection, an eternity of "ceasless change" (V, 182–183). In Eden, spring and fall "Danc'd hand in hand" (V, 395).

In the mortal world, as the speaker's similes repeatedly illustrate, nature's changes bring conflict, loss, danger, confusion (and it is suited to his special identity as blind bard that he so often thinks of confusion as the result of errors in *seeing*). Night's darkness bewilders travelers, stormy winds and waves threaten mariners, eclipses predict disaster to monarchs, volcanoes and earthquakes imperil nations. These qualities of experience are reflected even in human fables, and history and Scripture paint the same picture. Men's daily lives — the lives of shepherds, merchants, sailors, astronomers, warriors, rulers, subjects — are continually threatened by such changes. These are the fruits of man's Fall, which in the poem we witness happening to Adam, and in our own lives share with the blind bard.

It is significant that the largest number of similes spoken by the narrative voice occur in the first four books and in Book IX. It is in these parts of the poem, because they are largely devoted to events occurring before man's Fall, that the narrator's comparisons between Adam's world and ours are most pointed and most poignant, and in these portions the similes often take the form of negative comparisons which explicitly insist on contrast rather than likeness.

The contrast between the narrator's world reflected in the similes and the world of prehistory is a contrast between unity and variety, simplicity and multiplicity, order and conflict. The syntax of the negative comparison asserts the superiority of one term to another, asserts that Satan's armies were greater in number and prowess than any armies fabled in heroic legend, that Eden surpassed all gardens planted or imagined by men, that Eve was "more lovely fair/ Then Wood-Nymph, or the fairest Goddess feign'd" by mortal poets (V, 380–381). Yet the elaboration of the second term of the metaphor, the loving attention to detail in the extended and linked similes of the speaker, implies a less single-minded attitude than the syntax of the comparisons asserts.

The names, for example, which occur in such profusion in the narrator's similes, reflect the shattering of unity, like the proliferation of tongues in the story of Babel. The archetypes of the creation were splintered into separate and even conflicting fragments so that since the Fall we can only know particular places and identify ourselves by particular names, often with fierce hostility and pride. Yet these names have their own beauty — Vallombrosa, Etruria, Fesole, Fontarabbia, or Alcinous, Pandora, Proserpina, Ceres — and they evoke all the wealth of learning and feeling, the glamor and sympathy we associate with the world of poetry. By the Fall we lost the wholeness and harmony of divine beauty, but we gained all the varieties of mortal beauty, and this beauty of the particular is all the more lovely because it is mortal. Thus the narrator's preoccupation with times of day or season, with change and loss, again reflects a double attitude. We have lost Adam's innocent assurance of the permanence of the true pastoral world but we have gained the particular beauties of May and of autumn, the nostalgia that comes with evening, the glamor of moonlight, the hope of dawning. Even if these cycles of nature which rule our lives threaten us with danger, confusion, and inevitable loss, we would not change the color and movement, excitement and energy of this familiar world of trial, from which the narrator draws his comparisons, for the world of unfallen Adam, so fresh and untroubled and unchanging.

The shifting and divided world which the narrator's similes recall throughout the epic is the world of history stretching between the action of the poem and our own lives. The events of this world are described in the similes in the past tense, if they occurred uniquely — once in history — in the present if they are events which might occur at any time or inevitably recur again and again. For example, in the linked series of comparisons describing Satan's armies, which we have seen to be typical in its structure, content, and tone, the first comparison uses the present tense — the angels are like fallen leaves that "strow" the brooks (I, 302) — because autumn returns every years to Vallombrosa. The second comparison begins in a compound tense — the armies are like sedge scattered when Orion with his winds "hath vext" the Red Sea (I, 306) — because this is a recurring event, but then the time shifts to the simple past tense to tell of a particular moment in our distant history when the waves "orethrew" Busiris (I, 306). This manipulation of tenses in the speaker's similes, combined with his shifts of time in narrative and descriptive passages, reminds us continually of the mortal world from which we look back to the world of prehistory. We are never allowed to forget the immense gulf between these two worlds, an abyss of time as chaotic and impassable as the "Illimitable Ocean" (II, 892) dividing Hell from earth and Heaven. We look back through this history at the beginning of the poem as we look back to the time when the "Sons of *Eve*" gave names to the fallen angels catalogued by the speaker in Book I. We look forward with Adam through this history as it is revealed to him by Michael from the heights of Paradise.

The language of the catalogue of devils turned pagan gods is the same language as that used in the speaker's similes — sensuous, allusive, and particular. The narrator evokes his Muse to tell the "Names then known" (I, 376) of Satan's host but the verse is thickly textured with other names than those of the devils, identifications of people and places associated with the ancient history of our world:

> Next *Chemos*, th' obscene dread of *Moabs* Sons,
> From *Aroer* to *Nebo*, and the wild
> Of Southmost *Abarim*; in *Hesebon*
> And *Horonaim, Seons* Realm, beyond
> The flowry Dale of *Sibma* clad with Vines,
> And *Eleale* to th' *Asphaltick* Pool.
> *Peor* his other Name, when he entic'd
> *Israel* in Sittim on their march from *Nile*
> To do him wanton rites, which cost them woe.   (I, 406–414)

The historical authenticity of these names and places (described in the past tense because they are in the past of

reader and narrator although to the fallen angels they are
still in the future), the details which differentiate one god
from another or designate a particular vine-clad dale, give
reality to the fallen angels at the same time that they evoke
our sense of a rich and mysterious past. Specifications of time
and season create the same effects here as in the similes. We
recognize our own ephemeral world at the same time that
we sense its glamor when we are told:

> With these in troop
> Came *Astoreth*, whom the *Phœnicians* call'd
> *Astarte*, Queen of Heav'n, with crescent Horns;
> To whose bright Image nightly by the Moon
> *Sidonian* Virgins paid their Vows and Songs,
> In *Sion* . . .   (I, 437–442)

The complexity of feeling which informs the speaker's tone
is most fully illustrated by the passage which follows in the
catalogue:

> *Thammuz* came next behind,
> Whose annual wound in *Lebanon* allur'd
> The *Syrian* Damsels to lament his fate
> In amorous dittyes all a Summers day,
> While smooth *Adonis* from his native Rock
> Ran purple to the Sea, suppos'd with blood
> Of Thammuz yearly wounded . . .   (I, 446–452)

The logically superfluous allusion to a "Summers day," like
the startling adjective "purple," makes us feel the lush abun-
dance of the season and its inevitable passing. It affects us
like the evocations of seasons in the similes, or in the legend
of Mulciber of whom the fable says: "from Morn/ To Noon
he fell, from Noon to dewy Eve,/ A Summers day" (I, 742–

744) or in the blind bard's lament for the changing light of nature or sight of "Summers Rose." By these allusions the catalogue repeats the language of the narrator's similes and becomes itself a kind of super-extended simile contrasting our fragmented mortal world with the world of prehistory.

The history which we look back upon in the catalogue at the end of the poem we see carried up to our own time and then stretching before us in a prophecy of the future. In these last two books our world of danger, violence, vice, and confusion is most terribly envisioned by Michael but it is introduced by a passage of the speaker's which again directs our feelings about the mortal world. First the setting is described, the spot to which Adam and Michael have ascended:

> . . . It was a Hill
> Of Paradise the highest, from whose top
> The Hemisphere of Earth in cleerest Ken
> Stretcht out to amplest reach of prospect lay.   (XI, 377–380)

The tone of these lines suggests that the world which lies "all before" Adam is a glorious sight, far vaster than the "narrow bounds" of Eden (XI, 341). It is not merely spread but "Stretcht out," a verb more suggestive of animation and power, like the word "reach." The superlative "amplest" adds the sense of scope and abundance, while the possible double meaning of "prospect" as both "extensive view" and "future hope" increases the tone of anticipation.

This description is followed by one of the narrator's negative comparisons, one designed to support our hopes with a reminder that what was lost by Adam's Fall will be redeemed

in our future by the triumph of Christ, which occurred in
history between the events of the poem and the present in
which we read it:

> Not higher that Hill nor wider looking round,
> Whereon for different cause the Tempter set
> Our second *Adam* in the Wilderness,
> To show him all Earths Kingdomes and thir Glory.
>
> (XI, 381–384)

The next twenty-seven lines give a kind of second catalogue
of names, a list of places and rulers associated with the splen-
dor and power of our history:

> His Eye might there command wherever stood
> City of old or modern Fame, the Seat
> Of mightiest Empire, from the destind Walls
> Of *Cambalu,* seat of *Cathaian Can*
> And *Samarchand* by *Oxus, Temirs* Throne,
> To *Paquin* of *Sinæan* Kings, and thence
> To *Agra* and *Lahor* of great *Mogul*
> Down to the golden *Charsonese,* or where
> The *Persian* in *Ecbatan* sate, or since
> In *Hispahan,* or where the *Russian Ksar*
> In *Mosco,* or the Sultan in *Bizance,*
> *Turchestan*-born; nor could his eye not ken
> Th' Empire of *Negus* to his utmost Port
> *Ercoco* and the less Maritine Kings
> *Mombaza,* and *Quiloa,* and *Melind,*
> And *Sofala* thought *Ophir,* to the Realme
> Of *Congo,* and *Angola* fardest South;
> Or thence from *Niger* Flood to *Atlas* Mount
> The Kingdoms of *Almansor, Fez* and *Sus,*
> *Marocco* and *Algiers,* and *Tremisen;*

On *Europe* thence, and where Rome was to sway
The World: in Spirit perhaps he also saw
Rich *Mexico* the seat of *Motezume*,
And *Cusco* in *Peru*, the richer seat
Of *Atabalipa*, and yet unspoil'd
Guiana, whose great Citie *Geryons* Sons
Call *El Dorado*: but to nobler sights
Michael from *Adams* eyes the Filme remov'd . . .

(XI, 385–412)

The lines which introduce the passage and the punctuation which closes it seem ambiguous. When the speaker begins "His Eye might there command wherever stood/ City of old or modern Fame," the "Eye" might be Christ's, which would include the catalogue as part of the extended comparison, making the "sights" shown to Adam by Michael "nobler" than those shown to Christ by Satan. It seems equally possible that "His Eye" is Adam's and the list is not part of a simile but an actual description of the world before him, not as yet divided by names but capable of being described to mortal men only by such designations. Either reading supports the narrator's emphasis. The list is meant to dazzle us by the multiplicity of sounds and associations. Even more than the negative comparison of Satan's host to the armies of heroic legend, these names evoke impressions of mighty empires and boundless treasure. Yet the time sequence suggested in these lines never allows us to forget that although the empires named had not yet come into being at the time of Adam's vision — "*Rome* was to sway/ The World," Guiana was "yet unspoil'd" — now they are, despite their former power, past or passing, to become part only of the history of narrator and reader. This is the great world stretching before Adam, his future, but it is our past, for these empires are fallen, their wealth dispersed. The names are symbols then of our human condition, which Adam is to enter with the same doubleness of feeling that we share with the narrative voice.

The language of the similes and catalogues (if we may call this geographical list a kind of catalogue) characterizes the speaker in *Paradise Lost* as directly as the language of the abstract moral comments. To take either as alone representing the point of view of the narrative voice, of "Milton," is to reduce the tone to sentimentality or to complacency. It is because he is able to sustain this double vision, to combine the language of fallen men with the language of divine inspiration, that Milton's narrator can guide us by his "answerable style" to a true interpretation of the "higher Argument" of the poem. Only a speaker who shares our human nature could share our sympathy for Adam's passion and our response to its beauty. Only a speaker who shares our fallen condition could draw comparisons from the particular beauties of the seasons, of poetry, of history, and of daily life. Yet only a speaker whose mind has been illumined by heavenly inspiration could check our sympathy before it turned to sentimentality or measure our experience of particulars by an apprehension of divine truth. As bird or as blind bard, Milton's narrative voice can evoke the contrasts between the fallen and the unfallen world and by these contrasts raise our mortal imaginations to a vision of harmony illuminated by the inner light.

IV · SACRED METAPHOR

The narrator of *Paradise Lost* speaks a language of statement when he makes didactic comments interpreting his argument. He speaks a language of analogy when he uses similes to contrast the world of his own experience with the unfallen world of his poem. The particular, sensuous, and allusive language of the similes expresses the quality of changing experience which fallen reader and narrator share, as the directness and abstraction of the language of statement reflects the purity of vision granted to fallen man by the inspiration of the inner light. Both kinds of language are made appropriate in the poem because of the double nature of the narrative voice, whose capacity for both ways of speaking — for detailed response to multiplicity as well as apprehension of abstract truth — helps to create the unique tone of the epic.

The device of "author-comment" and the convention of extended simile were suggested to Milton by the epic tradition when he sought to transform the legend of Adam into a heroic narrative. It is characteristic that he should have exploited traditional devices and adapted them to the special needs of his argument and the special nature of his narrative voice. Yet his claim in the poem is not to have excelled in imitation but to have transcended tradition, to have surpassed all epic models and achieved a unique style capable of expressing "Things unattempted yet in Prose or Rhime."

This unique style is characterized by the combination of the language of statement and the language of analogy with still another kind of language which, with special modifications of meaning, may be called a language of metaphor.

Neither the didactic comments nor the epic similes are expressed in metaphors. The comments are phrased as abstract statements in a language almost entirely stripped of rhetorical figures, like the language of God. The similes are themselves figures, yet they insist upon contrast rather than identity; the more elaborately they develop the analogy between the familiar and the unknown the more we feel the chasm between the two worlds and the strangeness and mystery of both. Yet there is another kind of language, used most often for narration and description, which characterizes the narrative voice in *Paradise Lost* by its dependence upon a special kind of metaphor.

The opening invocation illustrates the way in which statement and analogy are combined with another manner of speaking which expresses the nature of the epic narrator. The "author-comment" on the intention of the speaker which concludes the invocation is stated in the direct, largely abstract, and nonfigurative language of the inner light, while the preceding allusions have the particularity of the language of analogy. But the opening summary of the plot illustrates still another manipulation of the language:

Of Mans First Disobedience, and the Fruit
Of that Forbidden Tree, whose mortal tast
Brought Death into the World, and all our woe,
With loss of *Eden*, till one greater Man
Restore us, and regain the blissful Seat,
Sing Heav'nly Muse . . .   (I, 1–6)

If this is a language of metaphor, it is of a special kind. For
these lines fulfill none of our expectations about the nature
of metaphorical style. They have none of the sensuous par-
ticularity, the concreteness, the multiplicity of connotations
expressing ambiguous or conflicting feelings, which Shake-
speare or Donne have led us to expect. The passage is a
formal, generalized, apparently nonfigurative restatement of
the historical events recorded in Genesis. The truth of their
history is assumed (this sin was the "First" in time and took
a particular form of disobedience to a particular prohibition),
as is our familiarity with the story and our acceptance of its
"Heav'nly" authority. The language of these lines also insists
not only on the particular historical reality of the people and
events in the poem but on their exemplary nature. The gen-
eralized diction of the opening summary tells us that this
particular event had universal significance. Here we do not
find people or places named as in the similes, times or seasons
specified. Adam is referred to simply as "Man"; his sin in-
fluenced the whole "World" and brought our common con-
dition of "woe."

The exemplary nature of Adam's story might at first tempt
us to read the passage as allegory rather than metaphor. The
particular event would then illustrate the general condition,
the concrete would represent the abstract, the thing be trans-
latable into the meaning. Yet these lines no more closely re-
semble what Spenser has taught us to think of as allegorical
language than they resemble the metaphorical styles of
Shakespeare and Donne. Milton's use of metaphor in fact
denies allegory, as the contrast between the first stanza of

one of Spenser's epic introductions and Milton's invocation
will illustrate. Book III of *The Faerie Queene* begins:

> It falls me here to write of Chastity,
>   That fairest vertue, farre aboue the rest;
>   For which what needs me fetch from *Faery*
>   Forreine ensamples, it to haue exprest?
>   Sith it is shrined in my Soueraines brest,
>   And form'd so liuely in each perfect part,
>   That to all Ladies, which haue it profest,
>   Need but behold the pourtraict of her hart,
> If pourtrayd it might be by any liuing art.[1]

It is first of all significant that in his epic introduction Spen-
ser discusses an abstract concept instead of telling a story.
The speaker's task here is to set forth the moral abstraction
"Chastity," distinguishing it from Queen Elizabeth or any
other particular figures, real or fictional, who could act as
"ensamples" to illustrate the moral conception. The meta-
phors from painting express the notion that the poet will
"write of Chastity" by painting a portrait of a particular
chaste figure who will illustrate his true argument, the nature
and excellence of the virtue itself. This initial distinction be-
tween abstract and concrete language tells us at once that we
are to read the poem as an allegory in which particular char-
acters and events act as rhetorical devices, as similes, illus-
trating abstract concepts; a poem in which descriptions of
places, characters, and events serve as images or speaking
pictures to illustrate moral conceptions. Although Spenser is
far from rigid, exclusive, or even consistent in his use of al-
legory, those sequences of *The Faerie Queene* which call

attention to their allegorical significance demand to be read in the ways suggested by the distinction of concrete and abstract in this introduction. This distinction is further supported throughout the poem by Spenser's most characteristic practice of linking an adjective suggesting abstract moral judgment with a noun representing a concrete thing (for example, from Book I, Canto 1, stanza i: "Gentle Knight," "mightie armes," "cruell markes," "angry steede," "iolly knight," "knightly giusts," "fierce encounters"). This device distinguishes objects from meanings by making particulars in the poem serve as illustrations of an independent scheme of abstract moral values. Allegory, like extended simile, therefore implies a separation between the terms it is apparently comparing, between the familiar and the unknown, the portrait and its conception.

Metaphor, on the contrary, insists upon unity rather than separation, identity rather than contrast. And Milton's language in the opening invocation is in a special way metaphorical, not allegorical, although the only *explicit* metaphor in these lines is the conventional identification of epic with song. This traditional metaphor suits Milton's style as Spenser's allusions to painting are appropriate to his allegory. For by identifying his poem with music rather than with painting, Milton not only allows for the metaphor of his poem as both the song of a bird and the epic of a blind bard. He also claims for it a special unity of meanings. The notes in a song do not stand for anything in the way that lines and colors in a painting can represent things which have reality outside the frame of the picture. The sensuous harmonies of music cannot be translated into abstract conceptions for which they serve as illustrations. Sound and meaning are indivisible in music, concrete and abstract are identified as they are in metaphor and as they are in the diction of Milton's opening invocation.

In the first five lines of *Paradise Lost* which summarize the argument there are a number of important words conveying both abstract and concrete meanings at the same time. "Fruit" means both "result" or "consequences" and "apple"; "mortal" signifies both "subject to death" and "human"; "tast" can be used to mean the general noun "experience" as well as the particular sensation associated with eating. By supporting both abstract and concrete meanings at once, the diction supports at once the particular historical reference of the story and its universal and inward meanings. Fact and meaning cannot be separated as they are in allegory. Each expresses the other in the unity of divine truth, so that the two references of a single word become the two terms of a metaphor by which their meanings are identified.

The diction of these lines therefore prevents them from being read as Spenser in many passages (especially ones which begin his episodes) tells us that *The Faerie Queene* must be read, even though to the twentieth-century reader, for whom Adam's story is a fable, it may be tempting to think of the concrete meanings of Milton's diction — the apple, the fatal act of eating, Adam whose very name is the Hebrew word for man — as allegorical inventions representing abstractions. To seventeenth-century readers, for whom Adam's story was sacred history, the interpretation of Genesis which Milton's language expresses was familiar, and the language itself — both general and in a unique way metaphorical — resembled the language of Scripture, in which concrete and abstract meanings are true and indivisible. This diction creates a variety of metaphor which is the only kind of figure appropriate to divinity. It is this language which the God of Milton's poem uses when, for example, he fore-tells the future state of fallen men:

> And I will place within them as a guide
> My Umpire *Conscience*, whom if they will hear,
> Light after light well us'd they shall attain,
> And to the end persisting, safe arrive.
> This my long sufferance and my day of grace
> They who neglect and scorn, shall never taste;
> But hard be hard'nd, blind be blinded more,
> That they may stumble on, and deeper fall;
> And none but such from mercy I exclude.   (III, 194–202)

The double senses of the words "light," "blind," "taste," "deep," "fall" used in this passage are exploited throughout the poem, in combination with other key words bearing double meanings in Christian theology — "head," "root," "fruit," "seed," "grace," "inspire," "illumine," "see," "dark" — to name only a few often repeated in *Paradise Lost*.

Not only the habits of language, but the specific interpre-tation of Adam's story which is assumed in the invocation to the epic was familiar to seventeenth-century readers, who recognized it as an orthodox reading of Genesis based upon a passage from the Epistle to the Romans: [2]

> Wherefore, as by one man sin entered into the world, and death by sin; and so death passed upon all men, for that all have sinned . . .
> Therefore, as by the offence of one *judgment came* upon

all men to condemnation; even so by the righteousness of one *the free gift came* upon all men unto justification of life.

For as by one man's disobedience many were made sinners, so by the obedience of one shall many be made righteous.

(Romans v:12, 18–19)

This interpretation of the Fall, which Milton assumed for his readers, depends upon the equation "all men were in Adam and Adam is in all men," an equation which is in itself a special kind of metaphor. For both terms, "Adam" and "all men," have concrete reality. Neither acts as a rhetorical device illustrating the other as, for example, in *Areopagitica* we understand the personification of the nun to be a figure of speech invented to depict abstract qualities of a "fugitive and cloistered virtue." [3] The words "Adam" and "all men" have equal concrete or historical reference and yet, unlike the names in the statement "Adam begat Abel," they are terms in a metaphor and both have abstract reference, both *mean* something in relation to each other and their meanings are identical with their concrete reality. To read either the passage from Romans or the invocation to *Paradise Lost* as allegory would destroy the meaning by dissociating particular facts from their spiritual or psychological values. In the unity of divine truth recorded in Scripture and apprehended by the blind bard, they are one.

The style of this invocation, with its general and nonvisual language (we are not made to picture an act of disobedience, an instance of woe, or the entrance of death into experience) and its simultaneous reference to concrete facts and their spiritual meanings, is uniquely answerable to Milton's argument and to his narrative voice.[4] Combined with the inspired language of statement and the fallen language of analogy, the language of metaphor expresses the blind bard's power to interpret "Things invisible" to our "mortal sight."

This style the speaker often uses to describe the places and characters in his story and to narrate its events. One more passage will serve as illustration here, the first description of Hell:

> At once as far as Angels kenn he views
> The dismal Situation waste and wilde,
> A Dungeon horrible, on all sides round
> As one great Furnace flam'd, yet from these flames
> No light, but rather darkness visible
> Serv'd only to discover sights of woe,
> Regions of sorrow, doleful shades, where peace
> And rest can never dwell, hope never comes
> That comes to all; but torture without end
> Still urges, and a fiery Deluge, fed
> With ever-burning Sulphur unconsum'd . . .   (I, 59–69)

As he does when he leads us into Eden, Milton's speaker is careful here to remind his readers that, although this is a description of the scene before Satan, it is not given in his language but the narrator's, who interprets Hell for us with powers divinely inspired beyond the limits of "Angels kenn."

First we are told that Hell is a "dismal Situation," a phrase which insists upon the identity of the concrete reality of the scene and its meaning.[5] A "Situation" is both a place and an inner condition; "dismal" means both "ill-omened" and also "depressing or threatening to the spirit." "Waste" is here used as an adjective meaning "sterile," "barren," but the distortion of syntax enables Milton to suggest at the same time the use of the adjective as a noun, "waste land." The phrase "Dungeon horrible" sounds like the beginning of one of Spenser's detailed pictorial descriptions but immediately all visual distinctness of outline is denied by the image of "darkness visible," an image which by its self-contradiction turns a sense impression into something like an abstract concept, swallowing all the details of the scene in the flickering of Hell's flames. Next the narrative voice gives a list of what the visible darkness "discovers," and again the verb means both the physical act of making known to the eye and the psychological act of revealing to the mind. The sights which are revealed have the same double references, even "doleful shades," which might seem like one of Spenser's pictorial images if "shades" merely meant "shadows" (although it is impossible to imagine what shadows would be cast by darkness visible). But again Milton's diction has more than one reference: "shades" also means "departed spirits," a reminder that our fallen vision of Hell is limited to its description in the epics of mortal poets whose fabled heroes descended to a feigned Hades. In contrast the Hell which this narrator "discovers" to us has the authority of divine truth.

The diction of this passage, with its double references, identifies the concrete and abstract meanings of the scene as they are identified in metaphor. It presents Hell as at once an area and a plight, a physical and a spiritual reality, and it insists on the unity of these two kinds of reality. There is no conflict between the two references of a single word, as there is for instance when Donne exploits a word which has both sexual and religious meanings. Nor do Milton's double uses of words here create the ironic plays of meaning that

Shakespeare characteristically achieves by using words which in their unique dramatic context express extraordinary combinations of feelings. The double references of Milton's diction are traditional and he uses them in traditional contexts, as metaphors expressing the unity of divine truth. This unity is interpreted for us by the blind bard who can transcend the fragmentary world reflected in the similes because his mind is illumined by the direct rays of the inner light. With his guidance we, though fallen, comprehend Hell as the fallen Archangel does not. We know the true meaning of Satan's claim that "The mind is its own place, and in it self/ Can make a Heav'n of Hell, a Hell of Heav'n" (I, 254–255). We know that the true meaning of this proposition cannot be that we freely create our own spiritual condition, autonomous and dissociated from God's creation, but that our spiritual "place" and our "place" in the order of being are identical, are interchangeable terms in a single metaphor. Hell is Satan's "lamentable lot" (II, 617), and only he does not recognize that his "lot" is both his inner fate and his environment, that these are one and inescapable.

The ritualistically repetitive use of words with more than one reference to express divine unity of vision is the most important characteristic of the narrator's metaphorical style in *Paradise Lost*. In part it explains a number of other devices of language which critics have traditionally observed and often attacked. Those who have admired these stylistic devices have most frequently defended them chiefly as means for Milton to increase the loftiness of his epic verse.[6] These devices do elevate the style, but it is perhaps more significant that, like the didactic comments and extended similes spoken by the narrative voice, these devices are *organic expressions* of the speaker's "great Argument."

In part the reliance on words with multiple meanings explains Milton's use of latinate diction which often bears such meanings, and his preference for the original Latin roots of words. The curious latinate adjective "orient," for example, which is often repeated in the epic, is useful to Milton because it bears meanings referring to appearance, movement, direction, and location. The narrator's first use of the word — to describe the banners of the fallen angels "With Orient Colours waving" (I, 546) — depends on its meaning "resplendent." More often the word is associated with the sun, whose "brightning Orient beam" (II, 399) purges hellish "gloom," another word exploited frequently in the poem for its multiple meanings. In association with the sun the word "orient" combines the meaning of "resplendent" with "rising," suggestive of the vast circular motions of nature's wheel, and also with "eastern," an adjective which evokes opulent and exotic connotations, as it does in the lines describing the gate of Heaven "thick with sparkling orient Gemmes" (III, 507) and the rivers of Eden "Rowling on Orient Pearl and sands of Gold" (IV, 238). With the meaning "eastern" we also associate the special sanctity of holy places that traditionally lie in the East. The most familiar because the most effective use of "orient" occurs in Eve's beautiful love lyric which the narrator reports to us. She praises the sun "When first on this delightful Land he spreads/ His orient Beams" (IV, 643–644). To make us feel the full force of the word, with its multiple meanings,

Milton surrounds it here with much simpler, commoner, monosyllabic words with which it alliterates (in much the same way that Wordsworth in "A slumber did my spirit seal" makes a setting for the Miltonic word "diurnal"). We hear "orient" therefore with special emphasis as it expresses the meanings of sunrise for unfallen man in Paradise: the sun perpetually circling the earth sheds upon man heaven's radiant light and its protective warmth, encouraging the rich growth of the "fertil earth." Eden itself is endowed with the multiple properties suggested by the word "orient," and Eden is the "state" of innocence, an area, and an inner condition.

Milton's use of double meanings as a way of expressing unified vision also helps to explain his liking for puns and word play.[7] Adam's frequent use of the words "sole" and "part" in his speeches to and about Eve, and her echoing responses, illustrate how Milton uses puns to support his metaphorical meanings. When Adam in the first line of his first speech calls Eve "Sole partner and sole part of all these joyes" (IV, 411), the echo of the word "soul" reminds us that they are one soul, and also that she is part of his soul, a principle within him.[8] We hear the same play of meanings when Eve addresses Adam as "O Sole in whom my thoughts find all repose" (V, 28) or later most clearly when Adam calls her "Sole *Eve*, Associate sole" (IX, 227). The play on "partner" and "part" recalls the creation of Eve from a part of Adam, an association confirmed by Eve's memory of Adam's first speech to her: "Part of my Soul I seek thee, and thee claim/ My other half" (IV, 487–488). The reiteration of these words with their combined double meanings seems

to foretell the real separation of Adam and Eve "That Morn
when first they parted" (IX, 848) and Adam's passionate
refusal to recognize that separation in his speech before the
Fall: "from thy State/ Mine never shall be parted, bliss or
woe" (IX, 915–916). The final ironic echo is heard when
Adam, addressing God who created Eve as His last, best
gift, blames his own disobedience upon "My other self, the
partner of my life" (X, 128).

Milton's dependence on words with more than one refer-
ence also in some measure explains his manipulations of
syntax. In the opening invocation of the poem, for example,
the distortion of "normal" English word order is effective,
in part, as a means of adding dignity and weight to the style
and suspending the sense through a sweeping verse para-
graph. In the first five lines, however, it is perhaps even more
significant that syntax is so manipulated that all the lines
end, with especially marked emphasis, in nouns, among
which are the key words in the passage bearing the simul-
taneous references to concrete and abstract realities. The
narrator's description of Satan gives a further illustration of
the way Milton's practice of widely separating subject and
verb can support the double references of his diction, in
addition to suspending the sense and animating the move-
ment of the passage:

> . . . he above the rest
> In shape and gesture proudly eminent
> Stood like a Towr . . .   (I, 589–591)

If the verb here were to come immediately after the subject
—"he stood above the rest"—we should tend to read this

passage only as a description of Satan's physical location or greater height above the other fallen angels. By separating "Stood" from its subject (in part by the intervention of words referring to moral qualities), Milton calls attention to the abstract as well as the physical meaning of the verb, and therefore makes it possible for us to read the passage at the same time as a description of Satan's physical and his inner condition. He is "above" his comrades in grandeur and pride as well as in form and location; "eminence" is his inner and outer "situation." Physical and psychological "height" are, by the manipulation of syntax, identified as terms in a single metaphor.

The oddness of the syntax, when Milton separates the two adjectives which modify a single noun, as in the phrase "vast profunditie obscure" (VII, 229), calls our attention to each of the words separately, so that we may be made aware of their multiple possibilities of meaning — of "profunditie" as both "deep abyss" and "abstruse concept," of "obscure" as physically "dark" or "gloomy" and also psychologically "remote" or "unknown." We are further prepared to attend to these meanings by the frequent earlier uses of the word "obscure," especially in another odd arrangement of words — the "palpable obscure" (II, 406) — in which the adjective, because it is turned into a noun, has properties interchangeable with the adjective now modifying it.

A number of other words like "obscure" are used in the poem as both adjectives and nouns. In the phrase "vast profunditie obscure," the word "vast" is used in its normal form as a modifier, but because it is separated from its fellow-modifier and contrasted so distinctly in sound with both "profunditie" and "obscure," we give the word "vast" here a special weight it would not have in a more conventional phrase such as "vast spaces." This adjective is also used in its familiar form in the phrase "vast abrupt" (II, 409), which here puts the emphasis on the peculiarity of the noun, but in the phrase the "vast of Heav'n" (VI, 203) we are made to feel the strange tangibility of Heaven's infinite spaces by the transformation of adjective into noun. A similar effect is created in Raphael's description of the creation of the firmament "In circuit to the uttermost convex/ Of this great Round" (VII, 266–267). The unusual use of "convex" and especially "Round" as nouns rather than as adjectives gives density and tangibility to *shape* itself; convex-ness and round-ness become primary qualities. Shape and mass, essence and attribute are identified in a unity which our habitual grammar divides. Less immediately striking, perhaps, but even more useful for Milton's purposes are his intricate manipulations of such words as "dark," which even in ordinary speech are used as either adjective or noun and which can refer to a spiritual quality or a physical fact. The simultaneousness of these references gives palpable existence to the quality and meaning to the fact. The same double use can be made of words which have noun and adjective forms, such as "gloom" and "gloomy," by which the speaker identifies the blackness of Hell with the spiritual misery of damnation.

The narrator's description of Satan in Hell illustrates still other manipulations of nouns and adjectives designed to identify concrete and abstract meanings and therefore to satisfy the special demands of the poem's "higher Argument" and of the blind bard's powers of vision. We are told, for example, that Satan witnesses "sights of woe" and "Regions of sorrow" (I, 64–65). By joining a concrete and an abstract noun in this fashion, Milton equates them; each borrows the properties of the other, like the terms in a metaphor. Sights in Hell are indistinguishable from the suffering which is their cause and effect, and woe is essential, palpable, almost visible. Sorrow becomes the element in which the fallen angels dwell, and the burning waste around them becomes one with their psychological suffering. The place is not an invention to depict the feeling, nor the feeling simply an explanation of the place.

The same effect is achieved in this description of Hell when we are told that Satan's eye discovered "huge affliction and dismay" (I, 57). This device of linking an adjective usually referring to concrete, physical qualities with an abstract noun has an effect the reverse of Spenser's most characteristic practice of linking an adjective conveying abstract moral judgment with a noun referring to a thing. Spenser's device actually seems to separate concrete and abstract meanings and to subordinate the thing to the concept which it illustrates, while Milton's equates the two. "Affliction" takes on weight and dimension in Hell, through the physical reference of the adjective "huge," just as, in the same phrase, the objective, externally imposed pain designated by the noun "affliction" is identified with the subjective, psychological pain implied by the noun "dismay" to which it is joined. Hell is a "situation," a "place," a "lot," a "state," both an area and an inner condition of suffering.

Milton's manipulation of adjectives and nouns creates still another effect antithetical to Spenser's most characteristic allegorical style. If, as in Spenser's typical combinations, moral values are expressed by the adjective alone, those values may at times seem subjective or relative or even arbitrary. When Spenser's narrator describes "steel" as "wicked" or a "quill" as "humble," we feel these values to be determined by the speaker and the situation. In some other context, "steel" might conceivably be "humble" and a "quill" be "wicked." Virtually any object, therefore, may in this kind of allegorical language be made arbitrarily to stand for any abstraction. Milton's peculiar combinations of adjectives and nouns and his repeated use of words with double references which may be used in either grammatical form create the opposite impression by insisting that essence and quality, thing and meaning, fact and value are identical, absolute, fixed in the nature of God's creation.

Milton's careful arrangement of the facts provided by his sacred story supports the metaphorical effect of his diction and syntax and reinforces the antiallegorical style of his epic. The effects of the arrangement depend on the fixed nature of the story, its authenticity as history, and our familiarity with it, as Spenser's allegory for the most part depends on the opposite possibilities of arbitrary connections, of fantasy and exaggeration, of suspense and mystification.

Milton's arrangement of narrative facts to create the effect of metaphor can be illustrated by the narrator's description of Satan's face as he surveys his fallen comrades:

Dark'n'd so, yet shon
Above them all th' Arch Angel: but his face
Deep scars of Thunder had intrencht, and care
Sat on his faded cheek . . .   (I, 599–601)

This description, like so many in the poem, gives us a general
impression rather than a sharply outlined picture. Our
response depends in part upon sense impressions — of Satan's
strangely dimmed luminosity as he stretches always above
us — but these visual and spatial impressions are as close to
an abstract concept as they are to a clear portrait. For we are
made to combine the ideas that "care," personified, had
marked Satan's face, with the concrete fact that his cheeks
also bear the scars made by thunderbolts. The combination
of the personified abstraction with the physical fact prevents
us from responding to the description simply as a picture,
as we are also prevented because in our ordinary experience
of the world of men, our notion of thunder and our notion
of a face are too disproportionate to fit together in a single
literal portrait. Our tendency, therefore, is to read the line as
an ordinary rhetorical figure: Satan's face is deeply scarred
by the kind of lines that tempestuous emotions and explosive
passions etch upon a human face. Thunder seems then to be
a rhetorical invention used in a metaphor to express the inner
turmoil of the ruined Archangel. Yet at the same time that
the difficulty of visualizing the description has encouraged
us to read the line as a rhetorical illustration, Milton has pre-
pared us by his arrangement of the facts of his sacred narra-
tive to read the description also as a literal statement. First
the narrative voice informed his readers how Satan was
"Hurld headlong flaming from th' Ethereal Skie/ With

hideous ruine and combustion" (I, 45–46), which suggests something like the blazing din of thunder and lightning. Then Satan consistently associated God with thunder, attributing His victory to the use of thunderbolts (I, 93, 258, 328). And the fables of mortal poets have already taught the reader to compare God's wrath to the terror and might of thunder hurled from the sky. Milton's narrator has also used descriptions and similes to give us a sense of Satan's enormous physical size, so that the reader feels the devil to be built on a scale capable of bearing the marks of thunderbolts, in scars like trenches ripped in the earth. Milton's reiteration of the facts of his narrative, the fact that God wreaks his anger in thunder and the fact that Satan's body extended "many a rood" (I, 196) above the height of mortal men, impels our acceptance of these facts. We are therefore led to read that "Deep scars of Thunder had intrencht" Satan's face as a literal statement at the same time that we read it as a rhetorical figure. The concrete term of the metaphor, thunder, is provided by the literal facts of Milton's divinely inspired story, and therefore has as much reality as the abstract term, the inner turmoil of the fallen Archangel, with which it is identified.

This arrangement of his narrative is the reverse of the allegorical method and reinforces the antiallegorical nature of the speaker's metaphorical diction. Spenser's method in allegorical sequences is to intensify the fantastic and magical details of his story, to exaggerate the arbitrary connections between events or objects and the concepts which they illustrate, in order that the reader may rise above a mere literal acceptance of the story to find its true, abstract meaning.

Milton's speaker, on the other hand, claims to retell sacred history in his epic and that history provides a world of tangible objects, of distinct figures and places, of predictable events from which the narrative voice draws the concrete terms for his true metaphors. We are made to feel that this world, and everything with which God filled it in the six days of creation, has the reality and meaning of divine truth in itself as well as metaphorical value for the abstract or inward meaning of the epic argument.

Even the most fantastic, the most magical details of the legend from Genesis are exploited in such a way that they support the narrator's literal language of metaphor and therefore deny the possibility of allegory. Perhaps the clearest illustration of this accommodation of argument and style is Milton's treatment of the creation of Eve.

In Genesis the creation of Eve is presented in the wonderfully matter-of-fact and succinct fashion characteristic of the legend as a whole. Scripture simply records:

> And the Lord God caused a deep sleep to fall upon Adam, and he slept: and he took one of his ribs, and closed up the flesh instead thereof;
> And the rib, which the Lord God had taken from man, made he a woman, and brought her unto the man.
>
> (Genesis ii:21–22)

In Genesis it is Adam who interprets the meaning of this event and draws from it a practical moral application:

> And Adam said, This is now bone of my bones, and flesh of my flesh: she shall be called Woman, because she was taken from Man.

Therefore shall a man leave his father and his mother, and shall cleave unto his wife: and they shall be one flesh.

(Genesis ii:23–24)

This passage was of course not only familiar to Milton's audience, but accepted by them as history. Yet it is his elaborate treatment of the event which enables him to exploit it as a metaphor in which both terms act as literal truths, whose meanings are both apprehended literally.

In *Paradise Lost* the miraculous creation of Eve is not reported as an event until Book VIII, when Adam to detain and interest Raphael tells it to the angel as the only story he knows. Yet there are references to it throughout the poem which the reader, knowing the Biblical story, recognizes. The earliest of these references is made by Eve herself, at the beginning of the first of her speeches reported by the narrative voice:

O thou for whom
And from whom I was formd flesh of thy flesh,
And without whom am to no end, My Guide
And Head . . .   (IV, 440–443)

Eve repeats the reference when in telling her story she reports the first speech Adam ever made to her:

. . . Return fair *Eve*,
Whom fli'st thou? whom thou fli'st, of him thou art,
His flesh, his bone; to give thee being I lent
Out of my side to thee, neerest my heart
Substantial Life, to have thee by my side
Henceforth an individual solace dear;
Part of my Soul I seek thee, and thee claim
My other half . . .   (IV, 481–488)

"Bone of my Bone, Flesh of my Flesh" (VIII, 495) is a kind
of refrain in the poem preparing us for Adam's passionate
reiteration of it as he joins fallen Eve in the fallen world of
woe:

> Should God create another *Eve*, and I
> Another Rib afford, yet loss of thee
> Would never from my heart; no no, I feel
> The Link of Nature draw me: Flesh of Flesh,
> Bone of my Bone thou art, and from thy State
> Mine never shall be parted, bliss or woe.   (IX, 911–916)

After the Fall Adam turns this refrain, with all the other
language which once expressed his innocence, against itself
in cynicism, mockery, and despair. He calls fallen Eve:

> . . . but a Rib
> Crooked by nature, bent, as now appears,
> More to the part sinister from me drawn,
> Well if thrown out, as supernumerarie
> To my just number found.   (X, 884–888)

Because we know the story and because it is treated as
sacred history, we accept these passages in one sense as
literal statements. Eve *was* formed of a rib taken from
Adam's left side; they *are* one flesh. Yet in another sense we
read these passages as metaphorical expressions of the inner,
psychological unity of Adam and Eve, as a figurative way of
describing their sexual and spiritual oneness. We cannot
visualize them as literally "one Flesh, one Heart, one Soule"
(VIII, 499) and therefore we respond to these passages as
metaphorical language saying that Adam and Eve are so
closely joined in the physical and spiritual harmony of
sanctified love that they are *as* one being. Both ways of read-
ing these passages are of course appropriate, as even the

characters in the poem recognize, for sacred events do express meanings, like terms in a metaphor.

Elaborating even more fully upon these few verses from Genesis, Milton included a detail in his narrative which would reinforce the meaning of Eve's miraculous creation. Until their fatal parting before the Fall, Adam and Eve are almost always described as "hand in hand" or embracing,[9] Eve often leaning upon the side from which she was taken as a vine leans upon a sheltering tree. It is only just before the Fall that the narrative voice says of Eve: "from her Husbands hand her hand/ Soft she withdrew" (IX, 385–386). Immediately after the Fall we are told that Adam "seis'd" Eve's hand (IX, 1037), but the violence and possessiveness implied by that verb are not qualified here as they are earlier when Eve describes how before their first union Adam's "gentle hand/ Seisd mine" (IV, 488–489). When the speaker tells us in the closing lines of the epic that Adam and Eve leave Eden once more "hand in hand," we feel with special emphasis that their oneness is re-established. The reiteration of this simple detail of physical description therefore reinforces the repeated references to Eve's miraculous creation so that we are made to feel the accumulation of metaphorical as well as literal meanings. These double meanings are further supported by diction consistently associated with Eve's creation which suggests concrete and abstract references simultaneously — "head," "heart," "part," "one," "state" — and by abstract and concrete words in combination.

The language of metaphor which Milton exploited in *Paradise Lost* was uniquely suited to the special nature of his argument and to the special nature of his invented speaker. It accommodated itself to epic style by its formality and its weightiness, and by its antiallegorical nature it was suited to express Milton's mature view of experience. For the whole energy of his mind was directed toward the search for unity, his language reaching always toward expression of the wholeness of experience. His insistence upon the sanctity of sexual love, his Mortalist doctrine that soul and body are indivisible even in death, his theory that the world was not created *ex nihilo* but from primal material, all his beliefs and habits of mind denied the division of spirit and matter, of physical and psychological experience, of fact and meaning, that Spenser expressed in his allegorical style. Milton's rejection of his earlier plans for an allegorical drama of the Fall was therefore a natural part of his development as a poet, his invented style in *Paradise Lost* an expression of his view of experience, his narrative voice the instrument for articulating that view.

The speaker uses a language of metaphor to describe the places and characters and events of his narrative. Unlike the language of statement or the language of analogy, this metaphorical language is limited, predetermined by the narrative itself. The language of statement, used in the didactic comments of the speaker, can draw its abstract judgments from the whole range of moral experience, can allude to the corrupting power of riches, the beauty of temperance, the sanctity of marriage, to any ethical knowledge appropriate to the poem's narrator. The language of analogy, used in the speaker's similes, can with even greater arbitrariness draw from all our mortal legends, our fallen history, our fragmentary daily lives the material for comparison and contrast with the unfallen world. But the meta-phorical language of *Paradise Lost* is defined by the limits of the poem's argument, because both terms of its metaphors must be drawn from the world of the poem. Both must have the authenticity of divine truth if they are to be simultane-ously meaningful and true.

Milton's language of metaphor in *Paradise Lost* therefore has a simplicity and clarity quite unlike the texture of Donne's or Shakespeare's figurative styles, or of his own metaphorical styles in *Comus, Lycidas,* or *Samson Agonistes.* The world from which the terms of Milton's metaphors are drawn in the epic is the world made by God in the six days of divine creation and described by Raphael to Adam in Book VII. This is a world of archetypes, of things appre-hended in their essences, and the only language to describe this world is a language of comparable clarity and gen-erality.[10] The words which create Milton's metaphors by their double references to abstract and concrete realities are not usually words designating secondary qualities. They are words which characteristically refer to essential conditions, to locations and durations, rather than to colors or shapes or surfaces. To emphasize their simple, primary meanings, they are stripped of extensive or conflicting connotations.[11] This kind of language is appropriate to the speaker, who is at the same time by his special nature also capable of ex-pressing his vision by statement and by analogy.

His metaphorical language is designed to recapture for us the unity which was shattered by the Fall of Adam. We are meant to feel in the poem that this unity is recreated by a kind of miracle, that without the presence of the inspired narrator interpreting the places and events of his poem, we would be incapable of envisioning the unity of the world of prehistory. We are therefore reminded continually of the difficulty of the speaker's achievement, its dangers, its inspired guidance, its uniqueness. And we are deliberately made to feel a kind of strain in the language of metaphor. The devices which support it are for the most part deviations from our ordinary uses of language or from the kinds of blank verse which Elizabethan drama has taught us to think of as our normal uses of language. Milton's particular, ritualistically repetitive exploitations of latinate diction, of words bearing more than one traditional meaning, and of roots of words are almost unique in English usage. The combinations of concrete adjectives with abstract nouns, of two nouns of different kinds, the use of adjectives as nouns, the syntax which is so often contorted to support more than one possibility of meaning, all these departures from conventional English practice stand out with marked distinctness in the language of *Paradise Lost*. We are not so forcibly struck with the numerous occasions when Milton uses the more conventional combination of abstract adjective and concrete noun, nor do we mark with any particular emphasis the lines which follow conventional syntax. The "normality" of so much of Milton's language is of course essential to the success of the poem and saves it from freakishness or whimsicality as well as from monotony. But it is not what gives the epic its special texture or makes us conscious of it as the unique achievement which the speaker claims it to be.

That claim rests partly on the uniqueness of the language of metaphor itself. For that language recreates our lost vision of a world now strange, awesome, distant but perfectly distinct. It is a world in which words perfectly identify things, as the names which Adam gave to the animals corresponded to their natures. It is a world of uninterrupted patterns of motion and unclouded light. It has the qualities of a wholeness, harmony, and radiance which are reflected in the metaphorical language of the narrative voice.

The language which recreates this world gives the epic the clarity of outline, generalized yet distinct, the cool luminosity which we associate with Milton's epic style. But that language is combined with the language of statement — bare, abstract, declarative — which gives the poem its austerity and firmness, and with the language of analogy, which contrasts the fallen world of the similes with the unity of the metaphorical world of the poem. The language of analogy contributes the richness of ornament, the denseness of allusions and conflict of impressions, the glamor and variety which we also associate with Milton's epic style.

These qualities are all to be found in *Paradise Lost*, and it is their unique combination which gives the epic its own uniqueness. Only a narrator like the blind bard could achieve all the kinds of vision, expressed in the comments, the similes, and the metaphors of *Paradise Lost*. Only by contrasting his own powers of vision with our darkened minds could Milton's speaker evoke our feelings of awe and nostalgia, fear and calm acceptance in response to his interpretation of the story of Adam's Fall.

V · ALLEGORY
AND PARODY

The language of metaphor in which the speaker reunites the fragments of truth shattered by man's Fall is not the language of the poem's fallen readers, who are made to feel in the verse that the unity is recreated by miraculous power, and it is not the language of the figures within the poem once they have experienced the disunity of sin. By contrasting the language of the narrator with that of his fallen characters, Milton again exploited the possibilities of narrative to develop the meanings of his epic.

The language spoken by Adam and Eve before the Fall reflects the special kind of metaphorical vision that also characterizes the narrative voice. Both they and the narrator speak in the language of Scripture, which assumes that because the world is an expression of the divine intelligence of its Creator, all the individual creatures in that world and all that happens to them express meanings. We are made aware of the resemblance to Scriptural language by frequent quotations and paraphrases of the Bible in both narration and dialogue, and by the almost ritualistic repetition of words which in Scripture and in the poem act as metaphors referring at once to physical and spiritual realities. Their constant reiteration gives them special emphasis, almost tangible outline and weight.

One illustration of this practice we have already seen. Adam and Eve before the Fall repeatedly use the language of Genesis to describe their union. Their reiterated references to the creation of Eve from Adam's side, their sense of unity in "flesh" and "bone," as one being, "parts" of one "soul," insist upon the simultaneous truth of the story as concrete, historical fact and as abstract, spiritual reality. The diction provided by Genesis refers to both meanings simultaneously.

Unfallen man's understanding of marriage coincides with the divinely inspired narrator's vision. His repeated observation of their literal union "hand in hand" or embracing, his hymn in praise of their wedded love, his comparisons of Eve's dependence on the "side" which gave her being to the dependence of a vine on a sheltering tree, reinforce in the narration the same Biblical metaphors spoken by the characters themselves.

The Fall, however, transforms the language of Adam and Eve as the feelings which that language embodies are changed by sin, until debased language in turn creates debased feelings. Fallen man no longer understands the sacred metaphors which the inner light has illumined for the blind bard. When, as we have seen, Adam after the Fall calls Eve "but a Rib/ Crooked by nature" (X, 884–885), his language reflects more than conscious cruelty. It reflects the division in fallen man's understanding between concrete fact and abstract meaning. Adam's words are effective as an insult because they assume now that a "rib" is in itself a *mere* thing, that is, an object without meaning or value of its own. Eve can recognize the insult because she shares this assumption; the same shattering of unified vision is earlier implied in her argument with Adam when she seems, almost like

Satan, to deny the facts of her origin as she has in act denied her dependence:

> Was I to have never parted from thy side?
> As good have grown there still a liveless Rib.
>
> (IX, 1153–1154)

To man's fallen understanding a rib is now a "liveless" thing, divorced from its meaning, no longer the term of a metaphor defining at once Eve's physical origin and her spiritual nature.

Although we the readers share this disunified vision in our own experience and therefore in our language, in the world of the poem we judge it as it is based upon misconception and as it expresses itself in sin. It is the speaker who guides our judgment, by direct statement and by similes. After their Fall, for example, he describes how Adam and Eve

> . . . each the other viewing,
> Soon found thir Eyes how op'nd, and thir minds
> How dark'nd . . .   (IX, 1053–1054)

The division expressed in their language is a reflection of their disunified experience. Having lost the inner light, they now move in darkness and so no longer share the vision of the narrator. In a simile he again implies that the sin which darkens their minds is the only true blindness:

> So rose the *Danite* strong
> *Herculean Samson* from the Harlot-lap
> Of *Philistean Dalilah*, and wak'd
> Shorn of his strength, They destitute and bare
> Of all thir vertue . . .   (IX, 1059–1063)

Like Samson and like Satan, they are shorn of their inno-

cence and the chief sign of their loss is their failure to appre-
hend the sacred metaphors that were once the key to their
experience. Their inward is divided from their outward
"state." [1] Now they stand in need of the divine illumination
which has restored unity of vision to the blind bard.

Our judgment of fallen man's understanding is further
controlled by reminders of its resemblance to Satan's. Dis-
sociation characterizes Satan's vision throughout the poem.
Habitually the fallen Archangel separates inner and outer
experience, thing and meaning, appearance and reality, fact
and value. All his words and actions express this division
from the opening scene. In his first speech, for example, he
changes facts to suit his own interpretation of them: God
rules only by superior force; Satan's followers were "In-
numerable"; the outcome of the battle was "dubious"; God's
strength is decreed by superior "Fate" (I, 84–124). Other
facts he denies or cannot recognize, refusing to admit the
reality of Hell or the effects of sin upon his own nature. His
inner confusion, like fallen man's, prevents him from appre-
hending the unity of divine creation, and his language, like
ours, perpetually divides things and meanings. It is only
Satan in the poem, for example, who says that mankind was
seduced from innocence by an "apple" (IX, 585; X, 487).
By using the word "apple" rather than the Biblical words
"fruit" or "root" with their double references — words which
God, unfallen man, and the narrator use over and over
throughout the epic — Satan implies that mankind was
tempted by a *mere* thing, an object of no value or significance
because without spiritual reference.

The confusions in Satan's language are immediately recognizable to the poem's readers, who are assumed from the opening invocation to be rational though fallen, to be lovers of truth and virtue, and to be familiar with Scripture and convinced of its divine authority. Guiding our response to Milton's particular interpretation of Satan, however, the speaker from the first scene directs us to think of Satan as a divided being, just as we are made to think of Adam's sin as the loss of the unified vision which characterized the state of innocence. "Semblance" in Satan's words and deeds is never true to "substance" (I, 529). Opposition, conflict, and contradiction characterize his fallen experience. Even in Hell, before his fallen comrades, his appearance and his inner life are in opposition, as they are in Eve when, after eating the forbidden fruit, she chooses how she will "appeer" to Adam (IX, 817), disguising the reality within her by false manners and lies. This is how we are told to measure Satan's first speech:

> So spake th' Apostate Angel, though in pain,
> Vaunting aloud, but rackt with deep despare . . .
>
> (I, 125–126)

The emphasis in these lines is on the conjunctions indicating contrast. The speech is meant to belie the inner experience and the comment to point out the power of the contradiction. Satan's words do not sound despairing precisely because the division within him is so serious. Only the inspired narrator can penetrate the appearance to discover the reality.[2]

Satan acts out this division in his experience by his deliberate attempts to make his outward appearance and actions belie the reality within him. His hypocritical behavior and his assumption of disguises, reflecting the same dissociation we hear in his language, are again interpreted by the narrator as the separation of inner and outer experience:

> Thus while he spake, each passion dimm'd his face
> Thrice chang'd with pale, ire, envie and despair,
> Which marrd his borrow'd visage, and betraid
> Him counterfet, if any eye beheld.
> For heav'nly mindes from such distempers foule
> Are ever cleer. Whereof hee soon aware,
> Each perturbation smooth'd with outward calme,
> Artificer of fraud; and was the first
> That practisd falshood under saintly shew,
> Deep malice to conceale, couch't with revenge . . .
>
> (IV, 114–123)

The diction here, with its emphasis on deep artifice and false creation (recalling Spenser's descriptions of the magician, Archimago), implies that the division which characterizes fallen beings is a violation of nature, that unity of being is the original state of all creatures as it was of Adam and Eve in Eden, Satan once in Heaven.

The language of Satan and of fallen man unnaturally disjoins the unities of God's creation, while the metaphors of the inspired narrator, so to speak supernaturally recreate those unities. This contrast is another means provided by narrative form for developing the poem's meaning. Yet there are some distinct portions of the poem which appear to deny all that has been said, portions in which the narrator uses a style closer to Satan's or to fallen Adam's, which seems antithetical to his metaphorical language because it insists on the separation of facts and values, the subordination of things to meanings.

The first instance of this kind of language spoken by the narrative voice occurs at the end of Book II in the meeting of Satan with the figures at Hell's gates. The episode begins with a description by the speaker:

> . . . at last appeer
> Hell bounds high reaching to the horrid Roof,
> And thrice threefold the Gates; three folds were Brass,
> Three Iron, three of Adamantine Rock,
> Impenitrable, impal'd with circling fire,
> Yet unconsum'd.   (II, 643–648)

The pointedly specific language and the precise enumeration of concrete details tell us that this description must be read differently from the narrator's first description of Satan's "Situation" in Hell. By insistently naming and differentiating and counting the physical facts of the scene, while repeating the traditionally magical number three, the narrator suggests that these facts stand for something beyond themselves, that concrete objects must here be translated into abstract meanings. Meaning is not *identified* with physical reality, as it is in the metaphors describing what the "darkness visible" discovers, but is *represented* by physical reality, as it is in allegory. We are at once made to see the scene and to feel that what we see must be transcended, or translated into an abstract meaning.

Our sense that this episode is to be read as allegory is supported by the introduction of the characters in the episode. Instead of naming these figures, recounting their history, or analyzing their moral nature, as the narrator has interpreted

the fallen angels to us, here he seems at first to be as ignorant
as Satan or the reader of the identity of these figures:

> Before the Gates there sat
> On either side a formidable shape . . .   (II, 648–649)

Immediately the speaker begins a detailed description of
their appearance and behavior, as if trying to learn, or mak-
ing the reader learn, who they are and what they mean
from how they look and act. The implication is that the
particular concrete details of their appearance and actions
will be translatable into the abstract moral significance of
these "shapes":

> The one seem'd Woman to the waste, and fair,
> But ended foul in many a scaly fould
> Voluminous and vast, a Serpent arm'd
> With mortal sting: about her middle round
> A cry of Hell Hounds never ceasing bark'd
> With wide *Cerberean* mouths full loud, and rung
> A hideous Peal: yet, when they list, would creep,
> If aught disturb'd thir noyse, into her woomb,
> And kennel there, yet there still bark'd and howl'd
> Within unseen.   (II, 650–659)

Unlike other descriptions in the poem, in which many of the
descriptive words have both concrete and abstract meanings
at the same time, this passage gives only the physical charac-
teristics of the female "shape," again reminding us of char-
acters in *The Faerie Queene*, especially of Errour, described
by Spenser's narrator as an "vgly monster":

> Halfe like a serpent horribly displaide,
> But th'other halfe did womans shape retaine,
> Most lothsom, filthie, foule, and full of vile disdaine.

And as she lay vpon the durtie ground,
Her huge long taile her den all ouerspred,
Yet was in knots and many boughtes vpwound,
Pointed with mortall sting. Of her there bred
A thousand yong ones, which she dayly fed,
Sucking vpon her poisonous dugs, eachone
Of sundry shapes, yet all ill fauored:
Soone as that vncouth light vpon them shone,
Into her mouth they crept, and suddain all were gone.

(I, 1, xiv–xv)

As in Spenser's passage, the details of the portrait of the
sight confronting Satan are descriptive of the monster's
physical identity, of sights and sounds. Only the adjectives
"foul," "mortal," "hideous" (and they are adjectives used
also by Spenser in his description of Errour) refer to moral
values or dimensions, attributed by the speaker to the physical
qualities. The effect is that produced by Spenser's typical use
of abstract adjectives to modify concrete nouns; the physical
detail is made to illustrate the moral judgment. This effect
is intensified because at the same time that we are made to
visualize the creature, we are also made to feel that what we
visualize is exaggerated, fantastic, not in itself literally true
but illustrative of some nonvisual, abstract meaning. We
therefore respond to the "shape" as to a rhetorical figure
invented to stand for some idea existing independently of
the figure itself. This feeling is substantiated by the narra-
tor's description of the second "shape":

The other shape,
If shape it might be call'd that shape had none
Distinguishable in member, joynt, or limb,
Or substance might be call'd that shadow seem'd,

For each seem'd either; black it stood as Night,
Fierce as ten Furies, terrible as Hell,
And shook a dreadful Dart; what seem'd his head
The likeness of a Kingly Crown had on.   (II, 666–673)

Again the description is of physical qualities. Moral evalua-
tions are implied only through the adjectives — "black,"
"Fierce," "terrible," "dreadful" — and the comparisons, while
the necessity of translating the physical into the moral mean-
ing is made clear by the speaker's efforts to intensify the
fantastic and mysterious qualities — "what seem'd his head"
— designed to illustrate abstract truths. We are not really
being asked to believe in the physical reality of this extraor-
dinary, disembodied monster, regarded even by the narra-
tor with bewilderment and surprise, but in the idea which it
was invented to represent.

This descriptive method is the reverse of the method
commonly used by Milton's narrator, as a comparison with
the first description of Adam and Eve will illustrate. Here
again the speaker introduces to us two figures assumed to
be strange to us:

Two of far nobler shape erect and tall,
Godlike erect, with native Honour clad
In naked Majestie seemd Lords of all,
And worthie seemd, for in thir looks Divine
The image of thir glorious Maker shon,
Truth, Wisdome, Sanctitude severe and pure,
Severe, but in true filial freedom plac't;
Whence true autoritie in men . . .   (IV, 288–295)

This is a description of the physical appearance of Adam
and Eve, yet here the language does not create a detailed

visual portrait. The only physical facts we are given are that these figures stand upright and that they wear no clothing, and it is not by concrete nouns but by adjectives — "erect," "tall," "naked" — that these physical facts are conveyed. In fact, the nouns naming their qualities have moral reference, as well as the other, more abstract adjectives. What we are told is that when we *look* at these creatures we actually *see* "Honour," "Majestie," "Truth," "Wisdome," "Sanctitude." These virtues have embodied reality as tangible as height or nakedness. Even when we are given more specifically visual details in the succeeding lines, we cannot separate them as mere illustrations of moral meanings. We are asked to believe in their literal physical reality as well as in the ethical truths with which these facts are identified:

> For contemplation hee and valour formd,
> For softness shee and sweet attractive Grace,
> Hee for God only, shee for God in him:
> His fair large Front and Eye sublime declar'd
> Absolute rule; and Hyacinthin Locks
> Round from his parted forelock manly hung
> Clustring, but not beneath his shoulders broad:
> Shee as a vail down to the slender waste
> Her unadorned golden tresses wore
> Dissheveld, but in wanton ringlets wav'd
> As the Vine curles her tendrils, which impli'd
> Subjection, but requir'd with gentle sway,
> And by her yeilded, by him best receivd,
> Yeilded with coy submission, modest pride,
> And sweet reluctant amorous delay.   (IV, 297–311)

Because of his lofty brow and "Eye sublime," because of the frequently abstract diction used to describe him and because of the firm sound of lines beginning and ending with accented syllables, we associate Adam — as we are told that we should — with the powers of the mind. His appearance and his nature are identical. Eve's beauty and the more "poetical," more mellifluous and figurative language used in her description cause us to associate her with powers of feeling and imagination which, as the vine depends upon the tree, require support from the reason and restraint by the judgment. Her inner being is inseparable from her form. Yet because concrete language is not subordinated to abstract language, as it is in the descriptions of Sin and Death or of Spenser's Errour, and because the description is not exaggerated in such a way that we reject its literal truth, we do not read the introduction of Adam and Eve as an allegorical description of Reason or Judgment and Feeling or Imagination. On the contrary, the speaker insists — his tone here expresses awe but not astonishment — that we believe in their historical reality, their physical presence, and at the same time he makes us recognize that their divinely created forms express moral meanings. Even Satan recognizes the outer and inner harmony of innocence, when he first sees Adam and Eve, and the fact that he does recognize it suggests both that he is still at moments capable of something like angelic vision and that their absolute unity of being is unmistakable:

> . . . so lively shines
> In them Divine resemblance, and such grace
> The hand that formd them on thir shape hath pourd.
>
> (IV, 363–365)

To describe unfallen man, even the fallen Archangel is

forced to use language which has at once physical and moral meanings: the outward "grace" of innocence is the visible sign of "grace" within. This metaphor is repeated when Raphael praises Adam's divinely created nature:

> Nor are thy lips ungraceful, Sire of men,
> Nor tongue ineloquent; for God on thee
> Abundantly his gifts hath also pour'd
> Inward and outward both, his image faire:
> Speaking or mute all comliness and grace
> Attends thee, and each word, each motion formes.
>
> (VIII, 218–223)

Repeatedly until the Fall, Adam and Eve are described by the words "grace" and "graceful" which, with their simultaneous references to physical beauty and spiritual virtue, identify the appearance of Adam and Eve and their moral natures as terms in a single metaphor. Their looks and actions cannot therefore be read in the way that we read the descriptions of the two monstrous "shapes" at the gates of Hell, as rhetorical inventions to illustrate allegorical meanings.

The impression of exaggeration and fantasy conveyed by the description of the "shapes" which Satan encounters in Hell is intensified in the story told to him by the female figure. The improbability of the events directs us to read the story allegorically, as we are prevented from reading Satan's history or the story of Eve's creation. And of course the suggestion that this story is a rhetorical illustration is finally confirmed by the naming of the monsters: they are concrete speaking pictures illustrating the abstract concepts of Sin and Death.

Language is used in this episode in ways antithetical to the metaphorical style of the speaker elsewhere in the epic. The methods of allegory are the reverse of the methods used earlier to convince the reader that Hell is an area as well as a plight, that Satan's immense size, mysterious luminosity, and superhuman sufferings are historically true as well as morally meaningful, that Adam and Eve are in form and spirit "graceful." Yet far from seeming simply an illustration of the "*confusion* of spirit and matter," of real and figurative, that Samuel Johnson criticized in the poem,[3] the contrast of allegorical and metaphorical language is so sharp, the episode itself, with its conclusion in Book X, so clear in its outlines and so distinctly set off from the rest of the narrative, that Milton seems to be making a point by the inclusion of this allegory. This contrast does not demand that within the episode every concrete detail, every image, every comparison must be translatable into an abstraction any more rigidly, exclusively, or consistently than they are to be translated in *The Faerie Queene*. The contrast demands only that the reader recognize and respond to a different mode of language and to insure this response Milton, like Spenser, takes particular care at the beginning of the episode to call attention by exaggerated means to his shift in style.

The inclusion of Sin and Death can partially be explained by the demands of Milton's Biblical material or his epic theory or his theological doctrine. The sanctity of the source for his narrative obviously prevented Milton from inventing characters or events not authorized by Scripture, yet the preface for poetic variety within epic unity encouraged him to elaborate the bare story from Genesis.[4] Allegorical abstraction was the obvious method by which he might include more characters and events without claiming to rewrite sacred history, and the precedent of other epic poets dignified this inclusion. The particular allegory also served the interests of his argument by illustrating two important points of doctrine. It illustrated that evil, though it may have the apparent glamor of Satan, is in reality as ugly as his offspring, and it also illustrated that the origin of sin is not in God, as Satan would have us believe, but in the perversion of the creature.[5]

These theoretical explanations for the inclusion of allegory, however just or relevant, do not preclude the possibility that Milton had other reasons more organically related to the essential nature of his epic. The beautifully sustained identity of the narrative voice elsewhere in the poem and the insistent way in which that voice calls the reader's attention to varieties of language, changes in point of view, and contrasts in ways of vision, suggests that here the shift to allegory in itself demands interpretation, as well as the abstract meaning which the allegory is invented to convey.

The very sharpness of the initial contrast between this episode and the rest of the poem first catches the reader's attention. The contrast between the reality of Satan, his followers, and his journey, and the abstractions of the allegory reinforces our sense of the historical truth and tangible physical existence of the other persons and places in the poem. We cannot reduce the fallen Archangel *as we are first made to see him* to an abstraction — Pride or Wrath or Despair or even Evil — because we cannot limit our response to him as to a rhetorical invention designed to illustrate a moral doctrine. We must admit Satan's superhuman qualities to be literally true, must feel that his actions did in fact transform our own history, precisely because we are made to see that his story is not an allegory feigned by a mortal imagination. The seemingly deliberate tension between antithetical uses of language, between sacred metaphors and allegory, which Dr. Johnson thought of as "confusion," is actually still another means of expressing the contrast between the inspired narrator's unified vision and the divided consciousness of fallen beings, which is at the heart of Milton's "great Argument."

In order to serve the larger meanings of the poem, Milton found it necessary to subordinate the allegorical material to the otherwise antiallegorical nature of his epic, instead of building the total poem within an allegorical frame, in the fashion of the morality play he had earlier planned to write. He chose consistently to limit his allegory to parts of the poem relating only to fallen experience, and this choice is in keeping with the traditional notion that allegory is one means of accommodating truth to the limited and darkened minds of men.

The one sustained allegorical episode in the epic is used to illustrate the origin and effects of Satan's Fall. It is also a representation of the nature of his vision and the quality of his experience, for although the story has to be told to Satan, as well as to the reader, it originated actually within his own mind, springing from his head with the figure of Sin. In introducing us to Sin and Death, the narrator is forced to use a mode of language different from that which expresses his own unified vision because he is describing the creatures of Satan's disordered imagination. These creatures do exist but they exist *as personified abstractions* and not as divinely created unified beings, and therefore cannot be described in sacred metaphors. The very fact that Satan does not recognize his offspring and has forgotten the act of her creation is a further illustration of his divided consciousness. This discrepancy between his inner and outer experience is expressed in the form of allegory, because the tendency which characterizes his fallen vision to disjoin physical and spiritual truths has its parallel in the allegorical method, which depends upon the separation of concrete and abstract meanings.

The language of the story told to Satan by Sin illustrates in the same manner as the narrator's allegorical description the meaningful connection between fallen vision and allegory.[6] The birth of Sin is a terrible distortion of Eve's creation, and the contrast between the allegorical language of this passage and the sacred metaphors which it parodies is the contrast between Satan's inner life and the vision shared by Adam and Eve before the Fall and by the inspired narrator:

> All on a sudden miserable pain
> Surpris'd thee, dim thine eyes, and dizzie swumm
> In darkness, while thy head flames thick and fast
> Threw forth, till on the left side op'ning wide,
> Likest to thee in shape and count'nance bright,
> Out of thy head I sprung: amazement seis'd
> All th' Host of Heav'n; back they recoild affraid
> At first, and call'd me *Sin*, and for a Sign
> Portentous, held me; but familiar grown,
> I pleas'd, and with attractive graces won

The most averse, thee chiefly, who full oft
Thy self in me thy perfect image viewing
Becam'st enamour'd, and such joy thou took'st
With me in secret, that my womb conceiv'd
A growing burden.   (II, 752–767)

Sin is born of the "left side" of Satan, but springs from his "head" as Athena was fabled to have sprung from Zeus, not from his "flesh" and "bone," and this birth is independent of God's creation. Sin's "attractive graces" are not, like Eve's "sweet attractive Grace" (IV, 298), a divine gift of inner beauty expressed in outward form, but the empty seductions of an abstraction. She is not of "one soul" with Satan but a kind of mirror reflecting his image, with which he became "enamour'd" as Eve might, like Narcissus, have been seduced by her own mirror image if she had not been completed by her union with Adam as one harmonious being. Yet Sin herself was seduced by Satan, as Eve will be in the temptation scene, a parallel underlined in a later passage in which Sin echoes Eve's dream and her temptation speech to Adam (X, 243–245).

Satan is the father of lies, the father of Sin, and, in a special sense, the father of allegory. The nature of his offspring which broke "violent way" from him is a revelation of the division in his fallen experience, and his history in the poem is his disintegration under the pressure of the widening division within him.[7] That disintegration is revealed in part by descriptions of Satan's changing appearance, his diminishing power and glory. The narrative voice foretells this decline in a description early in the poem:

> . . . his form had yet not lost
> All her Original brightness, nor appear'd
> Less then Arch Angel ruind, and th' excess
> Of Glory obscur'd . . .   (I, 591–594)

At intervals in the poem we are reminded of Satan's deterioration, as, for example, in a speech to him by the unfallen angel, Zephon:

> Think not, revolted Spirit, thy shape the same,
> Or undiminisht brightness, to be known
> As when thou stoodst in Heav'n upright and pure;
> That Glorie then, when thou no more wast good,
> Departed from thee, and thou resemblest now
> Thy sin and place of doom obscure and foule.   (IV, 835–840)

Even Satan himself recognizes his deterioration: "so much hath Hell debas'd, and paine/ Infeebl'd me, to what I was in Heav'n" (IX, 487–488).

That deterioration is also revealed in part by the sequence of Satan's disguises. First he assumes the radiant form of a "stripling Cherube" whose "feignd" outward "grace" (III, 639) belies the Hell within him, yet who belongs to the same order as Satan in the hierarchy of creation. The division between "semblance" and "substance" widens as Satan adopts the forms of animals — the cormorant, the lion, the tiger, the toad, and finally the serpent — until, in order to enter the serpent's shape, he even assumes a nonsensate state "Like a black mist low creeping" (IX, 180), formless and indistinct and itself a source of dangerous confusion. The truth that the sequence of his disguises is a descent of the chain of creation is recognized and lamented by Satan in his final speech before he enters the serpent:

O foul descent! that I who erst contended
With Gods to sit the highest, am now constraind
Into a Beast, and mixt with bestial slime,
This essence to incarnate and imbrute,
That to the hight of Deitie aspir'd . . .   (IX, 163–167)

The images of the speech explicitly call our attention to the
large pattern of Satan's decline, to his awareness of it, and to
its willfulness. He is "constraind" only by his own hatred;
his incarnation is a hateful inversion of Christ's.

The growing division within Satan is further marked by
the penetrating vision of the narrator, whose comparisons
of Satan to things which he resembles, as well as his direct
comments, describe the same general pattern of deterioration.
Satan in the beginning of the poem can fittingly be com-
pared to the mighty leviathan or to the sun, like Samson,
"Shorn of his Beams" (I, 596), to a comet, a griffin, or even
to Ulysses. But the Satan whose divided being assumes de-
basing bestial or nonsensate disguises can more fittingly be
compared to a vulture, a wolf, a thief, or gunpowder, or
swamp fire. The relation of the disguises to the similes as
reflections of Satan's deterioration is suggested by the use of
the same diction for both. When Satan sits "like a Cor-
morant" (IV, 196) or squats "like a Toad" (IV, 800) or
creeps "Like a black mist" (IX, 180) or crouches "as a Tiger,
who by chance hath spi'd/ In some Purlieu two gentle
Fawnes at play" (IV, 403–404), we cannot tell from these
formulas themselves whether Satan has actually disguised
the truth within him by assuming some other shape, or
whether the inspired narrator is in a simile describing to his
fallen readers the divided sensibility that their own distorted

vision would not otherwise discern. The lines about the tiger seem, in fact, to fuse a literal description with an extended simile. Not only the syntax but also the actual content of the similes often parallels the disguises: a cormorant is like a vulture, lions and tigers share qualities with the wolf, a mist resembles swamp fire.

The sequence of Satan's disguises marks the widening of the division within him until he degenerates into a figure in his own allegory.[8] When he assumes the disguise of a mist, he assumes a form like the allegorical figure of Death, black and shadowy, without shape or dimension. When he enters the body of the snake he makes himself like the "scaly" serpent, Sin. As Zephon declared, he has deteriorated into the likeness of his "sin and place of doom obscure and foule" (IV, 840). In Book X he again encounters his allegorical offspring but because he has knowingly committed himself to their world, this meeting is altogether different from their first encounter in Book II. Satan appears to them disguised "in likeness of an Angel bright" (X, 327), the form now a disguise which was once his true nature, yet his children are so united with him that they "Thir Parent soon discern'd, though in disguise" (X, 331). Satan on this occasion also recognizes his offspring because now he is truly "joyn'd in connexion sweet" (X, 359) rather than merely reflected in them, for he belongs to the same order of beings. It is fitting now that he go down the allegorical "Causey to Hell Gate" (X, 415) which they have built because the division in his nature is complete. He too is figurative now and the bridge carries him into the world of allegory. Even when his followers recognize him in a "shape" that recalls the Satan of

the beginning of the poem, that shape too is "false," a mere
appearance belying the reality within him:

> At last as from a Cloud his fulgent head
> And shape Starr bright appeer'd, or brighter, clad
> With what permissive glory since his fall
> Was left him, or false glitter . . .   (X, 449–452)

Like the figures of Sin and Death, Satan has no true "shape"
because he no longer belongs to the world in which physical
forms have both reality and meaning. He has become merely
a personification of evil:

>   . . . he wonderd, but not long
> Had leasure, wondring at himself now more;
> His Visage drawn he felt to sharp and spare,
> His Armes clung to his Ribs, his Leggs entwining
> Each other, till supplanted down he fell
> A monstrous Serpent on his Belly prone,
> Reluctant, but in vaine, a greater power
> Now rul'd him, punisht in the shape he sin'd,
> According to his doom . . .   (X, 509–517)

There is a beautiful fitness in Satan's fate, not simply in the
way the punishment is made to fit the crime, but also in the
way the style is made to suit his fallen condition. The lan-
guage of Satan's final speech reflects the completed division
of his consciousness:

>   . . . Him by fraud I have seduc'd
> From his Creator, and the more to increase
> Your wonder, with an Apple; he thereat
> Offended, worth your laughter, hath giv'n up
> Both his beloved Man and all his World,
> To Sin and Death a prey, and so to us,

Without our hazard, labour, or allarme,
To range in, and to dwell, and over Man
To rule, as over all he should have rul'd.
True is, mee also he hath judg'd, or rather,
Mee not, but the brute Serpent in whose shape
Man I deceav'd: that which to mee belongs,
Is enmity, which he will put between
Mee and Mankinde; I am to bruise his heel;
His seed, when is not set, shall bruise my head:
A World who would not purchase with a bruise,
Or much more grievous pain?   (X, 485–501)

Man offended for a mere "Apple"; God's judgment was only
on the "Serpent"; Satan's prize is a material "World"; his
punishment will be simply a "bruise." Physical reality is
totally sundered from moral meanings, things can only arbi-
trarily be made to *stand for* values (as money is made to
stand for the value of what it can "purchase"). It is fitting
that this dissociation overcomes Satan until his final doom is
that he cannot escape it. The dryness, the sterility, the ab-
straction of his fate is the inevitable conclusion to his de-
generation. The fallen Archangel has shriveled to a serpent
"constraind" within an allegory.

The allegorical language of the episode of Sin and Death,
the dualism which it reflects, and even the specific qualities
of the characters themselves are apparently intended to re-
mind us of Spenser's epic, which Milton once praised as a
moral poem.[9] The point here is not that when he wrote
Paradise Lost Milton had decided that Spenser's epic was
not a moral poem, but that in the context of his total vision
in *Paradise Lost* he uses allegory (among other literary
styles discussed below) as an example of fallen modes of

language. It is no more surprising that Milton, admiring Spenser and writing allegorically, should also criticize the mode itself than that in an epic he should both imitate and yet claim superiority to the heroic tradition, as in *Lycidas* he had used, questioned, finally transformed the conventions of pastoral for his own expressive purposes. In his poetry Milton characteristically assumes more than one attitude toward his literary models, claiming always a complex relation to the tradition in which he is writing. This characteristic doubleness of feeling is particularly expressive in *Paradise Lost* because it is voiced by the narrator who, as both fallen man and inspired bard, shares our attitudes toward the traditions of our mortal world and yet can view and judge them from a position which transcends our own. In this narrator's unified vision, allegory is identified with the dissociated vision of Satan; in this context allegory is presented as one of the forces which the devil let loose in the world.

By the equation of allegory with fallen vision in *Paradise Lost*, the episode of Sin and Death then becomes a kind of serious parody of what is presented as a false literary style. This intention is even clearer in the other, briefer and less serious allegorical episode in Milton's epic, Satan's visit to the Paradise of Fools. Here the connection between allegorical language and divided experience is also made more explicit, for the chief target of this parody is Catholicism, which, in Milton's presentation, is itself a kind of allegorical religion in which outward and visible objects are made arbitrarily to stand for inward and spiritual things. To the speaker this dualism results in "trumperie" by which the inner reality of things is "disguis'd" (III, 475, 480). Once things are divided from meanings, all that is left are the empty objects themselves:

>   . . . then might ye see
> Cowles, Hoods and Habits, with thir wearers tost
> And flutterd into Raggs, then Reliques, Beads,
> Indulgences, Dispenses, Pardons, Bulls,
> The sport of Winds . . .   (III, 489-493)

Catholicism is here Satanic because it is allegorical, and therefore the secondary target of this parody is again what is presented as the kind of false divisions expressed by allegorical language.

Satan as the originator of false vision is associated in the epic with other literary traditions implied to be falsifications of language. His very first speech identifies him as the creator of heroic poetry, the language of the "less heroic" epics which the speaker claims to surpass with his "higher Argument." Not only Satan's preposterous boasts of military prowess, but his exaggerated diction make this passage again a sort of parody. Within a single speech he summarizes the moral code which the narrator rejects as false heroism: "disdain," "power," "revenge," "hate," "courage," "Glory," "wrath," "might," "ignominy," "shame," "strength," "force," "guile" (I, 98–121). We recognize this rhetoric to be hollow, despite its glamor, because it is founded on lies, confusions, and deceit. Satan's heroic will we know to be dependent on the "high permission of all-ruling Heaven" (I, 212), and we hear how his final epic boast in the last address to his armies is answered only with "A dismal universal hiss" (X, 508).

He is the prototype of the mortal epic hero because as the father of false vision he is the inventor of false heroic values and false heroic language.

Satan's temptation speeches are the archetypes of still other fraudulent uses of language. His first speech to Eve, for example, is the archetype of poems in the courtly love tradition:

> Wonder not, sovran Mistress, if perhaps
> Thou canst, who are sole Wonder, much less arm
> Thy looks, the Heav'n of mildness, with disdain,
> Displeas'd that I approach thee thus, and gaze
> Insatiate, I thus single, nor have feard
> Thy awful brow, more awful thus retir'd.
> Fairest resemblance of thy Maker faire,
> Thee all things living gaze on, all things thine
> By gift, and thy Celestial Beautie adore
> With ravishment beheld, there best beheld
> Where universally admir'd; but here
> In this enclosure wild, these Beasts among,
> Beholders rude, and shallow to discerne
> Half what in thee is fair, one man except,
> Who sees thee? (and what is one?) who shouldst be seen
> A Goddess among Gods, ador'd and serv'd
> By Angels numberless, thy daily Train. (IX, 532–548)

Again exaggeration creates the effect of parody — here exaggeration of the servile tone and compression into a few lines of so many hyperbolic words and images typical of the language of courtly love poetry. This language has the "sleek enamel'd" quality of the serpent himself, and its falseness is particularly jarring in the simple, natural setting of the scene. It is meant to be contrasted with the archetype of the true love poem, which Eve recites to Adam in the scene in which she is introduced to us. Her complete submission to Adam is there expressed without hyperbolic diction or imagery because it is an expression of true metaphorical vision. Adam is her "Author and Disposer" (IV, 635) in both a physical and a spiritual sense. He is at once the center and the "head" of her world, as God is of Adam's. Love in this unfallen world does imply subordination as well as harmony because, like everything else in God's creation, it expressed divine order which is founded equally upon hierarchy and upon unity. But in the false flattery of Satan's courtly-love language, which still innocent Eve can recognize as "overpraising" (IX, 615), the sacred metaphors are sundered. Eve is elevated to a place above her proper rank by images — goddess, queen, saint, angel — which deny her true nature and her true "place." Elsewhere in the epic the narrator uses these images as ways of describing Eve: she is "Goddess-like" (VIII, 59; IX, 389), or attended "as Queen" (VIII, 60), or "Angelic" (IX, 458). The narrator in his true poetry uses these images as descriptive comparisons but Satan in his courtly-love language uses them as titles. He therefore turns images which are properly similes into metaphors, and by these false identifications destroys the true sacred metaphors. He divides Eve's outward "grace" from its inward meaning.

As a prototype of the fraudulent poet, Satan distorts language by falsifying images. As a fraudulent orator he originates the misuse of philosophical abstractions divorced from concrete references. The narrator prepares us for this parody by a simile, as earlier he prepared us for Satan's courtly language by describing the serpent's "turret Crest, and sleek enamel'd Neck" (IX, 525). Here the comparison of Satan's language with the tradition which he fathered is made explicitly:

> As when of old som Orator renound
> In *Athens* or free *Rome*, where Eloquence
> Flourishd, since mute, to som great cause addrest . . .
> (IX, 670–672)

Characteristically in this simile the narrator seems to dwell lovingly on the more familiar term of the comparison, exploiting the names of "Athens" and ancient "Rome" to evoke the golden age of human wisdom and power. Yet characteristically he also reminds us — here for example in the contrast with the present implied by the epithet "free Rome" — that in the fallen world wisdom fades and power is misused, a reminder which prepares us to accept Satan as the father of oratorical language which has the capacity to deceive as it persuades. His "great cause" is to make the worse appear the better reason, and his sophistical language again reflects his characteristically divided experience:

> O Sacred, Wise, and Wisdom-giving Plant,
> Mother of Science, Now I feel thy Power
> Within me cleere, not onely to discerne
> Things in thir Causes, but to trace the wayes
> Of highest Agents, deemd however wise. (IX, 679–683)

His address to the "plant" implies that the fruit itself has magical properties independent of God's will, and by calling it a "Plant" rather than "fruit" or "root," he severs its concrete reality from its abstract meaning. There are only two other occasions when the "fruit" or Tree of Knowledge is called a "plant." One occurs shortly after this speech of Satan's, when the narrator is ironically describing fallen Eve's obeisance to the tree "as to the power/ That dwelt within, whose presence had infus'd/ Into the plant sciential sap" (IX, 835–837). Here the word "plant" emphasizes the absurdity of Eve's idolatry and attributes it to the misleading power of Satan's false language. This connection is strengthened in Satan's pseudo-philosophical speech by the echo of the only other use of the word: the tempter's address to the "fair Plant" in Eve's dream (V, 58). Satan's description in his sophistical speech of the act of eating the fruit as a "petty Trespass" (IX, 693) implies that he has *merely* eaten an apple, that outward actions have no inward meanings. His concern is with "Science," with the "Causes" of "Things" and their "Agents," apart from their meaning as creations of the divine intelligence. His god is meaningless "Fate" (IX, 689), his aim knowledge divorced from morality, his philosophical position naturalistic and skeptical:

> The Gods are first, and that advantage use
> On our belief, that all from them proceeds;
> I question it, for this fair Earth I see,
> Warm'd by the Sun, producing every kind,
> Them nothing . . .   (IX, 718–722)

By refusing to recognize the spiritual realities of God's creation he destroys the distinctions of language which express the hierarchy of being. Here, as in his courtly-love speech, Satan does not give Eve her proper title — "woman" — the word used by Adam and the narrator to identify her physical

origin with her spiritual nature. In Satan's false philosophi-
cal language she is a "Goddess humane" (IX, 732).

As in allegory there is a division between concrete and
abstract, in parody there is a discrepancy between style and
subject, words and values. Parody, like allegory, is therefore
associated in *Paradise Lost* with Satan, because both depend
upon the divided nature of fallen experience. Yet it is essen-
tial to Milton's manipulation of narrative form that our un-
derstanding of these devices of language, and of the psy-
chological conditions which they represent, be controlled
by an elaborate pattern of contrasts between the world of
the poem's characters, the world of its narrator, and the
world of its readers. We measure the dissociations of the
allegorical language applied to Satan by its contrast with the
unified metaphorical style of the speaker, but because our
own vision has been distorted by the Fall, we can translate
the concrete facts of the allegory into the abstractions for
which they stand without the sense of strain with which we
apprehend the sacred metaphors illuminated for us by mirac-
ulous light. We recognize the falseness of the literary styles
which Satan originates because as they are presented in the
poem we are made to measure them by the language of the
narrator, unfallen man, angels and God. Yet Satan's speeches
are recognizable as parodies only because in our own world
we have interpreted our fallen experience by these same
kinds of literary language.

The total effect in the poem of these patterns of contrast
is ironic. Like allegory and parody, irony belongs to the
fallen world. To God in Heaven or to Adam in Eden there

can be no discrepancies between appearance and reality because inner and outer realities are one. The unified vision of unfallen beings therefore cannot be ironic, nor can the language of the narrator, in so far as he is inspired with a vision of the unfallen world, be itself ironic. Ironic effects in *Paradise Lost* are therefore not inherent in the diction, imagery, or tone of the narrator, in the ways that they characteristically are in the speaker's language in a Donne poem or a sonnet of Shakespeare's. Ironic effects in Milton's epic are created by the alternations in points of view made inevitable by the great fact of the Fall in which narrator, reader, and characters are all involved.

VI · VISION
AS STRUCTURE

The metaphors of *Paradise Lost* as the song of a bird or the vision of a blind bard emphasize the same qualities which Milton's speaker explicitly calls to our attention in his epic introductions: the uniqueness of the poem's argument and the distinctiveness of its form. The notes of a bird's song are peculiar to its kind, distinct from the surrounding scene and never translatable into other sounds, or into meanings other than their own. They form a pattern which has recognizable shape and one which stands out clearly against a formless background of unrelated noises, of accidental sounds. The vision of an inspired poet, cut off by blindness from the ways of other men, has also the uniqueness of its special meaning and its special form. A heavenly vision (and it is useful to Milton that the word means at once what is seen and the act of seeing) is not like other sights or ways of seeing. It is an internal sight which penetrates to "invisible" truths not equatable with our superficial knowledge, and it has a completeness of form, a wholeness of shape and clarity of design different in kind from our fragmentary impressions. Uniqueness of form in song or vision expresses uniqueness of meaning.

One of the strongest impressions which *Paradise Lost*

makes upon its readers is the impression of its remarkable
structure. When we finish the poem we feel that we can
almost *see* its shape.[1] It has completeness of form as if it
were itself a world, one which we could view in the way that
Raphael, looking down from the gate of Heaven, "no cloud,
or, to obstruct his sight/ Starr interpos'd," sees in the far
distance the shining globe of "Earth, and the Gard'n of
God, with Cedars crownd/ Above all Hills" (V, 257–261).
When we reach the final lines of the poem we have a view
of its total shape comparable to the view which Adam and
Eve have when they turn back to gaze on "Paradise, so late
thir happie seat" (XII, 642). One means of achieving this
effect is the device of placing the narrator by the side of a
character at a defined place in the world of the poem so
that we may gaze through his eyes at some other, distant
place. Or the narrator stands at a distance from the character
so that again with his aid we have a long view of the world
envisioned by the speaker. We therefore seem to be seeing a
complete shape; we gaze at the world of the poem as Galileo
studies the moon:

> . . . whose Orb
> Through Optic Glass the *Tuscan* Artist views
> At Ev'ning from the top of *Fesole*,
> Or in *Valdarno*, to decry new Lands,
> Rivers or Mountains in her spotty Globe. (I, 287–291)

Our inspired vision gives us an even more distinct and un-
shadowed view of the cosmos than

> . . . when by night the Glass
> Of *Galileo*, less assur'd, observes
> Imagind Lands and Regions in the Moon . . .
> (V, 261–263)

We are even privileged to see those places which, perhaps, "Astronomer in the Sun's lucent Orbe/ Through his glaz'd Optic Tube yet never saw" (III, 589–590). These comparisons express precisely our relation to the epic, as by their reiteration they help to create that relation. We see the structure of the poem and the world which it imitates as if we were looking through a telescope; [2] it has perfect shape, distinctness, coolness, and mystery. It is even, for the most part, seen in black and white. We view it with supernatural clarity and in some detail, yet never lose the sense of its total outline and vast distance from us.

The structure of the poem corresponds to the structure of the world which the narrator envisions,[3] and it therefore corresponds also to the peculiar nature and role of that narrator. Milton's "great Argument" demanded a poetic structure which would imitate the unity of the unfallen world. This structure was to make visible to the reader a world not to be known by any of our habitual means of knowing, because it was a world outside our familiar dimensions of time, space, motion, and light, a world which in its origins seemed impervious to change. To imitate this immortal world, as it is interpreted to the fallen reader by his inspired narrator, Milton employed the device of repetition, creating a structure at once unified and perfectly distinct.

Repetition, another of the epic conventions which Milton adapted to his own purposes, is one of the simplest and most obvious ways to make a point. Anything that is said over and over seems to grow in importance; the emphasis makes what is repeated seem to mean more than it might if it were presented only once. We have seen this device at work in

Paradise Lost in the meanings accumulated by the reiterated references to the story of Eve's creation. Repetition is also a simple and obvious way to suggest continuity, a state of things which either never varies, or varies only within an ever-recurring pattern. This method, we shall see, Milton uses in his presentation of Eden. But we shall also see that in building the structure of *Paradise Lost*, Milton characteristically exploits for his own special purposes these familiar forms of repetition to emphasize, to suggest associated or symbolic meanings, or to depict changeless states.

The pattern which recurs, seemingly infinitely, in *Paradise Lost* is the circle. This figure is especially suited to Milton's needs, as to Dante's, because it is a repeating pattern, turning endlessly upon itself, and because it is the traditional symbol of divine perfection, unity, eternity, infinity.[4] By building the poem in repeated circles, circles created by a variety of poetic devices, Milton imitated the form of the world envisioned by his inspired narrator.

The metaphors of the speaker as bird and as blind bard which Milton develops in his epic introductions serve, in addition to their other functions, to support the poem's structure by reiterating the pattern of the circle. This pattern is most fully elaborated in the opening of Book VII, the invocation to Urania whose voice the speaker has followed in his soaring "flight":

> Up led by thee
> Into the Heav'n of Heav'ns I have presum'd,
> An Earthlie Guest, and drawn Empyreal Aire,
> Thy tempring; with like safetie guided down
> Return me to my Native Element:

Lest from this flying Steed unrein'd, (as once
Bellerophon, though from a lower Clime)
Dismounted, on th' *Aleian* Field I fall
Erroneous, there to wander and forlorne.
Half yet remaines unsung, but narrower bound
Within the visible Diurnal Spheare;
Standing on Earth, not rapt above the Pole,
More safe I Sing with mortal voice, unchang'd
To hoarce or mute, though fall'n on evil dayes,
On evil dayes though fall'n, and evil tongues;
In darkness, and with dangers compast round,
And solitude; yet not alone, while thou
Visit'st my slumbers Nightly, or when Morn
Purples the East . . .   (VII, 12–30)

This passage occurs exactly in the middle of the poem, when
"Half yet remaines unsung." The metaphor of the narrator
in circular flight, compared here in a simile to Bellerophon's
terrible journey, recalls the earlier metaphors of the speaker
as a bird descending (like Orpheus and Aeneas) and ascend-
ing to the farthest reaches of the universe. Then, as in earlier
epic introductions, the metaphor shifts from the narrator
in flight precariously circling the heavens to the image of the
blind bard stationary in the center of his own dark world.
The invocation is the center of the poem's structure as Eden
is the center of its universe; we stand "on Earth" with the
speaker "Within the visible Diurnal Spheare." The structure
of the poem has narrowed from its vast inclusion of Heaven
and Hell to its concentration on "this punctual spot" of earth
(VIII, 23) and will widen again to include Heaven, Hell,
the past before the world was made and future to the end
of time, in imitation of the universe circling the place where

we and the speaker are "Standing." The device of locating
the narrator's angle of vision by specifying its relation to the
physical locations within the poem emphasizes the reality
of the shape of the world in the poem and its correspondence
to the form of the speaker's vision. The image of the narra-
tive voice as a bird ascending and descending in circular
flight therefore serves the structure of the poem because only
as a bird could he have physical presence in the farthest
reaches of the world of *Paradise Lost*. The repeated identifi-
cation of the speaker as a blind bard also contributes to the
circular structure of the epic. As a blind man the narrator
feels himself to be "compast round" by a hostile world re-
volving in darkness about his helpless head; but as inspired
poet the narrator feels himself at one with the great wheel
of nature, his mind illumined by the rotating lights of the
divinely ordained circle of creation:

> . . . yet not alone, while thou
> Visit'st my slumbers Nightly, or when Morn
> Purples the East . . .   (VII, 28–30)

Because the inspired narrator can apprehend the sacred
order of creation, he can make visible to us the structure of
this divinely unified world by the structure of his poem,
which is built upon almost endlessly repeated references to
the circling of the heavens around the little world of man,
the "Earth" on which the narrator stands in the opening of
Book VII. Every stage in the story of Adam and Eve is
marked by the speaker's allusions to the rotating of day and
night. When first we see this world, the narrator stands with
Satan looking down from "high above the circling Canopie/

Of Nights extended shade" (III, 556–557). Through his eyes we view the "golden Sun," lord over the "vulgar Constellations":

> . . . they as they move
> Thir Starry dance in numbers that compute
> Days, months, and years, towards his all-chearing Lamp
> Turn swift their various motions, or are turnd
> By his Magnetic beam, that gently warms
> The Univers, and to each inward part
> With gentle penetration, though unseen,
> Shoots invisible vertue even to the deep:
> So wondrously was set his Station bright.   (III, 579–587)

The soliloquy which Satan speaks once he has entered Eden is an expression of the torment stirred within him in part by the sight of the "full-blazing Sun,/ Which now sat high in his Meridian Towre" (IV, 29–30). Next we are presented with the narrator's vision of Eden and of Adam and Eve, which closes when the sun declines "and in th' ascending Scale/ Of Heav'n the Starrs that usher Evening rose." (IV, 354–355). After he has reported the first speeches of Adam and Eve and then Satan's response, the narrator reminds us again that nature's wheel is turning:

> Mean while in utmost Longitude, where Heav'n
> With Earth and Ocean meets, the setting Sun
> Slowly descended, and with right aspect
> Against the eastern Gate of Paradise
> Leveld his eevning Rayes . . .   (IV, 539–543)

Eve's love lyric and Adam's answering dissertation on the circling of the heavens are prepared for by what is perhaps the speaker's most beautiful description of nature's wheel:

> . . . now glow'd the Firmament
> With living Saphirs: *Hesperus* that led
> The starrie Host, rode brightest, till the Moon
> Rising in clouded Majestie, at length
> Apparent Queen unvaild her peerless light,
> And o're the dark her Silver Mantle threw.   (IV, 604–609)

As Adam and Eve retire we are told that they gaze above them at the "Moons resplendent Globe/ And starrie Pole" (IV, 723–724), and we leave them when night has measured "Half way up Hill this vast Sublunar Vault" (IV, 777). Finally Book IV ends with Satan's flight from Eden "with the shades of night" (IV, 1015), and immediately Book V opens with the speaker's traditional epic image:

> Now Morn her rosie steps in th' Eastern Clime
> Advancing, sow'd the Earth with Orient Pearle . . .
>
> (V, 1–2)

The wheel of nature surrounding man has come full circle.

All the scenes in Eden are described by the narrator according to this pattern. The action of Books V through VIII begins when the sun "With wheels yet hov'ring o're the Ocean brim,/ Shot paralel to the earth his dewie ray" (V, 140–141); it all takes place within a single day which is measured by the "mounted Sun" (V, 300) circling over the heads of Adam and the angel until Raphael observes that the setting sun "Beyond the Earths green Cape and verdant Isles/ *Hesperean* sets, my Signal to depart" (VIII, 631–632). The tragedy of the Fall in Book IX is introduced by a description of the descent of darkness:

The Sun was sunk, and after him the Starr
Of *Hesperus*, whose Office is to bring
Twilight upon the Earth, short Arbiter
Twixt Day and Night, and now from end to end
Nights Hemisphere had veild the Horizon round . . .
                                                    (IX, 48–52)

Inexorably the wheel of nature turns, "sacred Light" dawns
again in Eden (IX, 192), and within one revolution of the
circle the fate of mankind is sealed "while day declin'd"
(X, 99). The narrator's last allusion to the circling of the
heavenly bodies around the world of man nostalgically in-
troduces the scene of judgment which seals the end of the
true pastoral world:

Now was the Sun in Western cadence low
From Noon, and gentle Aires due at thir hour
To fan the Earth now wak'd, and usher in
The Eevning coole . . .   (X, 92–95)

These reiterations by the narrative voice recreate the pat-
tern of nature in the structure of the poem itself. They re-
peat a number of words for the same figure: "sphere,"
"globe," "orb," "arch," "wheel." They describe cyclical move-
ments: "rise," "climb," "ascend," "mount," "descend," "fall."
They reiterate patterns of sound, especially soft vowels and
combinations of *l* and *r*. Assonance and alliteration support
manipulations of syntax, especially the characteristic Mil-
tonic separation of subject and verb, to create in these pas-
sages the effect of movement suspended in an arc. For ex-
ample, in the lines "Now Morn her rosie steps in th' Eastern
Clime/ Advancing, sow'd the Earth with Orient Pearle" (V,

1–2), the separation of "Morn" and "sow'd" is emphasized by the contrasting vowel sounds of the intervening words, while the completion of the cyclical movement is stressed by the echo of the *o* in "Morn" which we hear when we finally reach the verb "sow'd."

All these passages use the same simple, generalized diction and traditional imagery which reinforces the fact of their repetition so that we feel the unending recurrence of un-fallen nature's changes. Here the narrator describes nature in the pastoral terms in which it appears to unfallen Adam and Eve and to the angels, not the terms which he charac-teristically employs in his own extended similes. In Eden each rosy dawn introduces the same day; each evening the sun slips into the ocean ushering in the same twilight, the same coolness, the same birds' songs. Changes in times of day are not associated with particular places or seasons or situations, as they are in the fallen poet's similes. Even the most specific adjectives which the narrator uses to describe nature's changes — "western," "eastern," "orient" — evoke the whole circle of the universe rather than any particular location.

The circular structure created in part by the narrator's circular repetitions is reinforced by still other uses of repeti-tion in the poem. The characters refer to nature's changes as often as the narrator and in the same language. The similes of Raphael and Adam, we have seen, draw comparisons from the round of the pastoral day. Raphael begins his nar-ration to Adam with an explanation of universal motion (V, 577–582) and throughout his story of the war in Heaven he marks the sequence of events by the rotation of morning and evening. In his description of the creation, he elaborates upon the motion of the spheres that revolve "on Heav'ns great Axle" (VII, 381) to serve as signs "For Seasons, and for Dayes, and circling Years" (VII, 342). Even the Milky Way is a "circling Zone . . ./ Pouderd with Starrs" (VII, 580–581). Adam begins his story to Raphael with a reference to the climbing sun (VIII, 255) and ends it with an allusion which completes the cycle:

> . . . the amorous Bird of Night
> Sung Spousal, and bid haste the Eevning Starr
> On his Hill top, to light the bridal Lamp.   (VIII, 518–520)

Eve greets her last day in Eden when the morn "begins/ Her rosie progress smiling" (XI, 174–175). Even Satan recognizes the circular order of God's creation, with Eden and man at its center:

> Terrestrial Heav'n, danc't round by other Heav'ns
> That shine, yet bear thir bright officious Lamps,
> Light above Light, for thee alone, as seems,
> In thee concentring all thir precious beams
> Of sacred influence: As God in Heav'n
> Is Center, yet extends to all, so thou
> Centring receav'st from all those Orbs; in thee,
> Not in themselves, all thir known vertue appeers
> Productive in Herb, Plant, and nobler birth
> Of Creatures animate with gradual life
> Of Growth, Sense, Reason, all summ'd up in Man.
> (IX, 103–113)

The circling of the heavens alluded to throughout the poem by its characters and its narrator is actually discussed at length by Adam and Raphael in Book VIII. The astronomy lesson has as its subject the "Wheele/ Of Day and Night" (VIII, 135–136). It is inspired by Adam's desire to understand the moral meaning of the "diurnal" round which he had earlier described in answer to Eve's more personal question: for whom do the stars shine when we sleep (IV, 667–668). Although the debate between alternative astronomical theories is left unresolved, the discussion itself supports the structure of the poem, because the angel insists that "Whether the Sun predominant in Heav'n/ Rise on the Earth, or Earth rise on the Sun" (VIII, 160–161), the physical order of the universe is circular, and man is its moral center (VIII, 85–100). The circular structure of the universe, in the center of which the narrator stands to report Raphael's lesson to us, is therefore a sacred metaphor of which the circular structure of *Paradise Lost* is a vision.

The astronomy lesson is a discussion of the wheel of creation; the morning song of Adam and Eve is a hymn in its praise. An elaboration upon Psalm 148, the hymn has its own key image, the "Perpetual Circle" (V, 182) of God's creation. Adam and Eve rejoice that the heavens are caught up in the circle of perfection; angels, stars, sun, moon, planets, air, and elements revolve in "ceaseles change" about the throne of God. The "Rising or falling" of waters, the ascent of birds imitate the cyclical order of the world. The principle of hierarchy, the scale of nature, becomes one with the principle of unity. Both are expressed in the figure of the circle, no rhetorical image invented by man for the purposes of his poetry, but a description of the actual arrangement of creation. The language of the hymn is literally descriptive at the same time that it is metaphorical; it corre-

sponds to Satan's actual view of the constellations dancing
round the sun or Raphael's comparison of "invisible" an-
gelic motion to the familiar movements of the heavenly
bodies that Adam has seen with his own eyes:

> Mystical dance, which yonder starrie Spheare
> Of Planets and of fixt in all her Wheeles
> Resembles nearest, mazes intricate,
> Eccentric, intervolv'd, yet regular
> Then most, when most irregular they seem . . .   (V, 620–624)

The shape of the universe in *Paradise Lost* is clarified by
still another repeated device. Distance in the poem is meas-
ured by lines within circles, "As from the Center thrice to
th' utmost Pole" (I, 74), and angelic characters travel within
these circles so that we feel even the space in Milton's uni-
verse to be curved as it is in Einstein's. Standing apart with
the narrator so that we can view through his eyes the whole
world of the poem, we see figures circling the heavenly
spheres or flying from circumference to center of the uni-
verse:

> . . . *Uriel* to his charge
> Returnd on that bright beam, whose point now raisd
> Bore him slope downward to the Sun now fall'n
> Beneath th' *Azores*; whither the prime Orb,
> Incredible how swift, had thither rowl'd
> Diurnal, or this less volubil Earth
> By shorter flight to th' East, had left him there
> Arraying with reflected Purple and Gold
> The Clouds that on his Western Throne attend . . .
>   (IV, 589–597)

The movement of the angel through the spaces between

the heavenly bodies gives tangible reality to their spherical shapes and cyclical movements.

Satan's flight from Hell through Chaos to the realms of light measures the height and depth of the universe of the poem; he rises from "bottomless perdition" (I, 47) to a height within view of "th' Empyreal Heav'n, extended wide/ In circuit" (II, 1047–1048). Even he is contained within the circle of creation, but we are made to see how characteristically his fallen understanding divides the moral meaning of nature from its physical order by exploiting the rotation of day and night to serve his own evil purposes. Satan turns darkness, which for unfallen Adam is a source of kindly rest, into yet another disguise to hide his dangerous machinations. The association of Satan, the "Prince of Darkness" (X, 383), with night is a metaphor in which both terms are literally true and meaningful. His purposes are "dark," and he keeps in dark places:

> By Night he fled, and at Midnight return'd
> From compassing the Earth, cautious of day,
> Since *Uriel* Regent of the Sun descri'd
> His entrance, and forewarnd the Cherubim
> That kept thir watch; thence full of anguish driv'n,
> The space of seven continu'd Nights he rode
> With darkness, thrice the Equinoctial Line
> He circl'd, four times cross'd the Carr of Night
> From Pole to Pole, traversing each Colure . . .   (IX, 58–66)

As the narrator warns us that the climax of the Fall approaches, we strain to watch Satan circling closer and closer to the center of the creation and the epic structure. Once on earth, the "Orb he roam'd/ With narrow search" (IX,

82–83), drawing his net more closely around unwary man until he constricts his motions to the "Circular base" of the serpent, lordly and commanding "Amidst his circling Spires" (IX, 498, 502). Eve's doom is sealed, and with hers, ours and the narrator's, when she is surrounded by the narrowest circle of all. Finding her alone and unsupported, Satan exploits the serpent's lovely shape "and of his tortuous Traine/ Curld many a wanton wreath in sight of *Eve*,/ To lure her Eye" (IX, 516–518). These ensnaring wreaths we know will "lure her Eye," even as Adam's circlet of roses, so soon to wither unregarded, can never please her now.

Here at its climax, and throughout the poem, in the center of its structure, action, and interest, are Adam and Eve. They are the center both of its Ptolemaic physical order and of its divinely intended moral order. Their relationship until the Fall is itself an unbroken circle whose symbol is the wreath of roses which was to crown Eve with the undying blossoms of the true pastoral world. The embraces by which they are "Imparadis't in one anothers arms" (IV, 506) imitate this circle of unity. The metaphor of Eve as a vine repeats the figure, for as the vine curls around the tree trunk, she depends upon Adam as the center of her world. Even her language revolves in circles around him, as her loveliest speech, her archetypal love poem, will illustrate:

> With thee conversing I forget all time,
> All seasons and thir change, all please alike.
> Sweet is the breath of morn, her rising sweet,
> With charm of earliest Birds; pleasant the Sun
> When first on this delightful Land he spreads
> His orient Beams, on herb, tree, fruit, and flour,

Glistring with dew; fragrant the fertil earth
After soft showers; and sweet the coming on
Of grateful Eevning milde, then silent Night
With this her solemn Bird and this fair Moon,
And these the Gemms of Heav'n, her starrie train:
But neither breath of Morn when she ascends
With charm of earliest Birds, nor rising Sun
On this delightful land, nor herb, fruit, floure,
Glistring with dew, nor fragrance after showers,
Nor grateful Evening mild, nor silent Night
With this her solemn Bird, nor walk by Moon,
Or glittering Starr-light without thee is sweet.   (IV, 639–656)

Beginning and ending with "thee," her poem revolves around Adam in an unbroken circle of repetition upon repetition. The last seven lines repeat in reverse and in the negative the first eleven lines. Within the poem individual words are repeated — "all," "sweet" — and they are words which recur especially often throughout the rest of the epic.[5] Word patterns are repeated exactly — "nor . . ." six times in five lines — or repeated in reverse: "Sweet is the breath of morn, her rising sweet." Patterns of sound are repeated within the love poem, especially soft *f*, *s*, and *r* sounds which elsewhere throughout *Paradise Lost* are associated with "fair" Eve's "sweetness" and "grace." By this association Milton suggests that the qualities of pastoral nature are the qualities of Eve. She is as "sweet" as the morn (to which Adam, who rarely uses similes, twice compares her), as "soft" as showers, as "fair" as the moon. Throughout the poem her inner and outer natures are described by these adjectives (which characteristically have both concrete and abstract meanings), and she is also repeatedly associated with the image of the moon as she personifies it here. Like the moon, she is queenly in her natural beauty, attended by a train of "winning Graces" (VIII, 61). Like the moon, she reigns in "peerless" majesty (IV, 608), a similarity which the tempter exploits when he suggests that like the moon when all creatures sleep, her beauty is unregarded (V, 44; IX, 546). Yet her light is a lesser reflection of the greater light of Adam's reason, her sun. The relationship which she acknowledges in her love song is paralleled in the circular movements of the sun and moon in the heavens, as they are later described by Raphael:

> . . . less bright the Moon,
> But opposite in leveld West was set
> His mirror, with full face borrowing her Light
> From him, for other light she needed none
> In that aspect, and still that distance keepes .
> Till night, then in the East her turn she shines,
> Revolvd on Heav'ns great Axle, and her Reign
> With thousand lesser Lights dividual holds
> With thousand thousand Starres, that then appeer'd
> Spangling the Hemisphere . . .   (VII, 375–384)

Like the moon, Eve is part of this circle of creation, her relation to Adam its center, so that the circular shape of her poem is itself a kind of metaphor for its meaning. Eve's language follows the pattern of her relationship to Adam, and that relationship is a microcosm of the world of which they are the center. As her world turns upon Adam, the heavens and the seasons rotate around the earth. Their benevolent purpose Adam explains to Eve in the speech which follows her love lyric. By attributing to the heavenly spheres a "kindly" intention of "Ministring" to nations (IV,

660–674), Adam reveals his understanding that their physical power to enlighten is an expression of the moral design of the creation. With the unclouded vision of innocence he sees, as the inspired narrator by his epic structure enables us to see, that the circular order of the universe and the circle of divinely established moral order are terms in a single metaphor.

By repeating these ever-narrowing circles the narrator imitates the world of his "higher Argument" in the shape of his epic; but that argument includes the great fact of the Fall which destroys the unity of the unfallen world and shatters its benevolent order. In Books IX and X we see each of the concentric circles broken in succession as a result of disorder in the innermost circle.[6] Eve places herself in the center of her world so that her language revolves around "I" rather than "thee"; she denies her nature as the moon reflecting the beams of the sun or as a vine curled around a supporting tree: "And what is Faith, Love, Vertue unassaid/ Alone, without exterior help sustain'd?" (IX, 335–336). Adam, no longer the center of Eve's circle, by subordinating himself to her forgets in turn that God is the center of his world. Eve by Satan's flattery is transformed into a false goddess, a Circe, and Adam, turned irrational, becomes her victim. By this overthrow of order both the hierarchy and the unity of their marriage are destroyed.

This disorder in the inmost circle destroys all the larger circular patterns. Not only do storms, thunder, cold, and heat shatter the seasonless round of nature, but the actual circular orbits of the heavens are interrupted. Either the angels, at God's command, "with labour push'd/ Oblique the Centric Globe" (X, 670–671) or else "The Sun, as from *Thyestean* Banquet, turn'd/ His course intended" (X, 688–689). Eclipses — which have earlier in the poem been associated, like all other interruptions of nature's course, only with the world of the narrator's similes — occur now in the physical world of the poem. When Sin and Death fly at Satan's bidding to wreak their destruction on earth, we are told:

> . . . they with speed,
> Thir course through thickest Constellations held
> Spreading thir bane; the blasted Starrs lookt wan,
> And Planets, Planet-strook, real Eclips
> Then sufferd.   (X, 410–414)

When Adam and Eve awaken on their last morning in Paradise, ironically consoled by the expectation of nature's wheel continuing to circle round them, the narrative voice warns us that they are mistaken:

> . Nature first gave Signs, imprest
> On Bird, Beast, Aire, Aire suddenly eclips'd
> After short blush of Morn . . .   (XI, 182–184)

Adam himself observes with fear the untimely "Darkness ere Dayes mid-course" (XI, 204). The eclipse becomes a symbol for the shattering of nature's cycle, the transformation of benevolent order into frightening unpredictability.

Because the argument of *Paradise Lost* included the Fall as well as the creation, division as well as harmony, mortality as well as eternity, the structure of the poem had to express not only unity but division, conflict, contradiction. The de-

vice of repetition was therefore not alone sufficient to answer
the structural demands of Milton's epic.

To imitate in the form of his poem the destruction of unity
Milton employed the device of contrast. This device is most
obvious as it involves the major places and persons of the
poem: Hell is contrasted with Heaven and both with Eden;
Satan is contrasted with Christ; Sin with Eve. These large
contrasts are, as we have seen, worked out in smaller pat-
terns. The story of Sin's creation is a parody of Eve's, her
union with Satan and Death a hideous distortion of Eve's
sacred oneness with Adam as well as of Christ's oneness with
the Father. Satan's council of revenge and his voluntary
"sacrifice" is a hateful inversion of the Council in Heaven
and the infinitely loving sacrifice of Christ for the redemp-
tion of fallen humanity. The stormy fires and ice of Hell
are the opposite of Heaven's calm radiance, the changeless
eternity of damnation the reverse of immortal life. Even
minor physical details are paired in contrasts: the causeway
leading to Hell and the chain to Heaven, the golden pave-
ments of Heaven and the glittering vaults of Hell.

More subtle are the contrasts between mankind and nature
as they are before and after the Fall. As we have seen, all the
qualities of unfallen experience are reversed by the "mortal
tast" of sin. In appearance — their "wonted Ornaments now
soild and staind" like Satan's (IX, 1076), in behavior, in lan-
guage, in their relationship to one another, Adam and Eve
after the Fall are contrasted with their lost condition of in-
nocence. The same contrasts are inevitably reflected in na-
ture, whose "calme Region once" becomes "tost and turbu-
lent" with tempests and eclipses that reflect in the greater

wheel of nature the "high Passions" and "Discord" within the innermost circle of man's soul (IX, 1121–1126). Contrast is also at work from the beginning of the poem between the mortal world which we share with the narrator and the world of prehistory envisioned in his poem. Only he experiences both worlds; the pattern we have seen most elaborately expanded in the contrasts between the world reflected in the speaker's similes and the world apprehended in his divinely inspired metaphors is designed to make their differences visible to us.

As the structural device of repetition in *Paradise Lost* is controlled by the figure of the circle, the use of contrast in the structure of the poem is also dominated by a key set of images, the contrast of light and dark. In the world of the poem this contrast is reflected in gradations from the pure effulgence of Heaven to the blackness of Hell.

When we read *Paradise Lost* we are most immediately impressed by the extremest contrasts of light and dark, flashing in alternation with changes of scene and place. These large patterns are built up by innumerable uses of opposing sets of words associated with opposing places and persons in the epic. Hell and its inhabitants are described by adjectives which are at once appropriate to night and expressive of melancholy or grim emotions: "black," "dark," "dreary," "dismal," "deep," "doomed," "gloomy." The frequent reiteration of these words, with their harsh consonant and deep *o* sounds, intensifies our sense of the physical and moral "darkness" of damnation. With Heaven and the angels we associate particularly the word "bright," contrasting in both meaning and sound with the descriptions of hellishness.

This word is used most commonly as an adjective but, like the word "dark," it is also used as a noun, as in the description of divine radiance "Dark with excessive bright" (III, 380), a device which makes the attribute of brightness a primary quality of celestial being rather than a secondary quality in the eye of the beholder. By reiterating such opposing words, images, and sounds, Milton depicts the conflict of forces within the unity of creation, which is the argument of his epic.

Conflict between Heaven and Hell, God and Satan, "bliss" and "woe" is fittingly expressed in the poem by absolute contrasts of light and dark imagery, for God and the devil are absolute opposites. Conflict as it is introduced by Satan into the divinely created order of man's world is expressed most often by a different device of language: the manipulation of various meanings of a single word or conflicting associations with a single image. This device is appropriate to depict the unique position of earth at the center of the world between Heaven and Hell, not the source of absolute light or darkness but the battleground where the great forces of light and darkness meet.

Eden, we have seen, is always described by the narrator in relation to the rotating wheel of light and darkness. In Hell there is no day, in Heaven no true night, but only "grateful Twilight" (V, 645) ushered in for "change delectable, not need" (V, 629). On earth there are recurring alternations and differentiations which meet in the word "shade." The meaning of the word itself implies the possibility of contrast because it implies the simultaneous presence of both light and darkness. An object can cast a shadow only if it stands in the path of light, and the quality of shadow itself is not absolute blackness or brilliance but dimness, half-light. These shadowy contrasts are expressive of earthly existence,[7] not of Heaven or Hell, the "state" of perfect "bliss" or utter "woe." When, for example, Satan lands in the orb of the sun, the narrator describes for us how he gazes down upon this world:

> . . . farr and wide his eye commands,
> For sight no obstacle found here, nor shade,
> But all Sun-shine, as when his Beams at Noon
> Culminate from th' *Æquator*, as they now
> Shot upward still direct, whence no way round
> Shadow from body opaque can fall . . .   (III, 614–619)

This unobstructed, unshaded view is possible for us, who see with mortal eyes, only because it is envisioned for us by the illumined mind of the speaker. With our own eyes, unaided, we see as through a glass darkly, and in our own world every light casts a shade.

The word "shade" in its variety of forms occurs throughout *Paradise Lost*, but it is used with pointed frequency and emphasis in the narrator's descriptions of Eden until it grows in meanings with the effect of a sacred metaphor. When first we enter Paradise we see above us:

> Insuperable highth of loftiest shade,
> Cedar, and Pine, and Firr, and branching Palm,
> A Silvan Scene, and as the ranks ascend
> Shade above shade, a woodie Theatre
> Of stateliest view.   (IV, 138–142)

Here the word is used most simply to mean "shade tree," and by its repetition gives the effect of density so that the trees themselves become like shadows, as well as casting them. The same effect is achieved later in this opening description. Nature, we are told, strewed flowers:

> Both where the morning Sun first warmly smote
> The open field, and where the unpierc't shade
> Imbround the noontide Bowrs . . .   (IV, 244–246)

Again the word suggests both the shape which casts the shadow and the shadow itself. The same effect is created when we are told that Adam and Eve sit down "Under a tuft of shade that on a green/ Stood whispering soft" (IV, 325–326), or when Eve describes how she first awoke to find herself reposing "Under a shade on flours" (IV, 451).

A "shade" is a protection, a benevolent source of comfort and refreshment. These associations accumulate with the repetition of the word. Descriptions of Eden are full of references to the "shadie Lodge," "shadie arborous roof," "shadie Woods," "shadie Bank," "shadie nook," "shadie Rivulet." We are also told that Eden is a place of "Walks and Shades," "Flours and Shades." The word "shade" is especially associated with the bower of Adam and Eve from the first identification of it by Uriel to Satan:

> That spot to which I point is *Paradise*,
> *Adams* abode, those loftie shades his Bowre.   (III, 733–734)

Adam leads Raphael where his bower "Oreshades" them (V, 376); its roof, we learn, is "inwoven shade" (IV, 693), and "shadie" is the commonest adjective associated with it as a kind of epic epithet. The implications of this association are expressed in one of the narrator's negative comparisons:

In shadier Bower
More sacred and sequesterd, though but feignd,
Pan or *Silvanus* never slept, nor Nymph
Nor *Faunus* haunted.   (IV, 705–708)

"Shadie" in Eden means not only cool and protected but
"sacred" and "sequesterd"; the bower is a place apart — holy
and private.

By this constant repetition of the word in both adjective
and noun forms, the narrative voice identifies Eden with the
qualities associated with "shades"; it is a region holy, re-
freshing, benevolent, protected. The same associations ac-
cumulate around unfallen man, appropriately, since Eden
is a "state" of innocence, both a place and a condition. Just
as the trees and the bower form a sheltering roof above man,
or the "pendant shades" (IV, 239) hang over him protect-
ingly, Adam "Leaning half-rais'd, with looks of cordial
Love/ Hung over" the sleeping form of Eve (V, 12–13).
The association of Adam with the sheltering "shades" of
Eden is made explicit in his warning to Eve before the Fall·

. . . leave not the faithful side
That gave thee being, stil shades thee and protects.
                    (IX, 265–266)

The metaphor is repeated in the narrator's description of Eve
alone in the Garden as the "fairest unsupported Flour,/
From her best prop so farr, and storm so nigh" (IX, 432–
433). Eve is also associated with the "shades" of Eden in
another metaphor. When first we see her we are told that
her golden tresses hang "as a vail down to the slender waste"
(IV, 304), a symbol of the "modest pride" which like a

"shade" shields her naked innocence. When she appears "Undeckt" before the angel Raphael, the narrator comments: "no vaile/ Shee needed, Vertue-proof" (V, 383–384). When Satan first spies her separate from Adam she is "Veild in a Cloud of Fragrance" (IX, 425) which seems to surround her innocence almost like an Homeric cloud. But the Fall destroys all that guards her and Adam:

> . . . innocence, that as a veile
> Had shadow'd them from knowing ill, was gon,
> Just confidence, and native righteousness,
> And honour from about them, naked left
> To guiltie shame hee cover'd, but his Robe
> Uncover'd more.   (IX, 1054–1059)

In a single metaphor the narrative voice here identifies the loss of innocence with the loss of "veils" and "shades," an identification repeated by both Adam and Eve when they lament the loss of Eden's pastoral "Shades" (X, 861; XI, 270).

Satan is the cause of this destruction and his opposition to the benevolence of God's creation is expressed from the beginning of the epic in part by his connection with different meanings and associations for the word "shade." One way in which the conflict in the world of the poem is imitated in the structure of the poem is by the contrasts of these meanings and associations with those of unfallen man and inspired narrator.

In the opening scene of the poem, Satan is associated with the "doleful shades" of Hell (I, 65). Here the noun, as we have seen, suggests not only shadows but ghosts, departed spirits mourning the loss of the world of light. This double meaning is again associated with Satan when he flees from Eden "Murmuring, and with him fled the shades of night" (IV, 1015). Not only darkness flies with him from Paradise but danger personified as malevolent spirits, attendants of the hostile kingdom of night. This definition of "shade" as malevolent ghost is used to refer to Satan's offspring, Death (X, 249), but his epithet is more commonly "Shadow," recalling the Biblical metaphor, the "shadow of death" (II, 669; IX, 12; X, 264). This meaning of the word is contrasted with its meaning for unfallen Adam and Eve. They know nothing of evil spirits, insubstantial but venomous, threatening them in the benevolent world which surrounds and protects them. To them "shade" means the substantial object, the tree, and also the effect of the tree, the coolness and shelter which it gives, while "shadow" means merely a reflected image or copy (IV, 470; V, 575; XII, 233). Yet the narrator knows, and by his contrasting language about Satan warns us, that evil exists and is active from the beginning of the poem, that a terrible threat hangs over man, hidden in those very "shades" of Eden which seem simply to shield and refresh him.

The opposition of Satan to the state of innocence is expressed not only by his connection with contrasting meanings of the word "shade," but also with contradictory associations for the same definition that it has for unfallen Adam. In the world of Hell surrounding Satan, nothing offers protection or refreshment; in the world of Hell within him nothing is endowed with benevolent or comforting intention. To him all gradations of darkness are themselves sinister or can be used for sinister purposes. In Hell the rebel angels find only "shades of death" (II, 621). In Heaven they fight in "dismal shade" (VI, 666) and are opposed by Christ's warriors spreading "thir Starrie wings/ With dreadful shade" (VI, 827–828). In Eden Satan is associated with night and darkness, when he can best accomplish his "dark" purposes. He seeks the protection of the "shades" to hide him or to disguise him, again sundering a sacred metaphor by dividing the moral meaning of protection from the physical fact of cool dimness. When he is discovered lurking in Eden, he escapes from the sight of Gabriel by fleeing "under shade" (IV, 572). When "Like a black mist" he makes his "midnight search" for the serpent whose form he will assume, he finds him:

> Not yet in horrid Shade or dismal Den,
> Nor nocent yet, but on the grassie Herbe
> Fearless unfeard he slept . . .   (IX, 185–187)

Not until Satan accomplishes his purposes is there any "horrid Shade" in Eden, any fear or any need for hiding places. When the devil goes to seek his victims in the Garden, the narrator in one of his direct comments laments the existence of danger where innocent Eve perceives only beauty and protection:

> O much deceav'd, much failing, hapless *Eve*,
> Of thy presum'd return! event perverse!
> Thou never from that houre in Paradise
> Foundst either sweet repast, or sound repose;
> Such ambush hid among sweet Flours and Shades
> Waited with hellish rancor imminent
> To intercept thy way, or send thee back
> Despoild of Innocence, of Faith, of Bliss.   (IX, 404–411)

Before the Fall, to innocent eyes the "shades" of Eden seem as sweet and as harmless as flowers, but sin brings knowledge of hatred, of danger, of fear, and in every shadow lurks the possibility of evil. Despoiled of the "veil" of innocence, fallen man seeks Satan's element of darkness, alienated by sin from heavenly light. These are the images in which Adam laments his Fall:

> How shall I behold the face
> Henceforth of God or Angel, earst with joy
> And rapture so oft beheld? those heav'nly shapes
> Will dazle now this earthly, with thir blaze
> Insufferably bright. O might I here
> In solitude live savage, in some glade
> Obscur'd, where highest Woods impenetrable
> To Starr or Sun-light, spread thir umbrage broad,
> And brown as Evening: Cover me ye Pines,
> Ye Cedars, with innumerable boughs
> Hide me, where I may never see them more.   (IX, 1080–1090)

The sheltering "shades" of Eden have become impenetrable "woods" or dark "glades." What God created for man's protection fallen Adam seeks as a hiding place from God. Like Satan, he has become an enemy of light. Instead of retiring for rest to the "sacred shades" of his bower, he hides "in gloomiest shade" to escape the judgment of God and the miseries of life (X, 716). Satan's conflict with innocence has filled Eden with the "shades" of Sin and Death, and night in Paradise has become like Hell, "with black Air/ Accompanied, with damps and dreadful gloom" (X, 847–848).

Like the structural device of circular repetition, the contrast of light and dark is suited to Milton's epic narrator and is supported by the metaphors of the bird and the blind bard.

The sacred bird tunes its "nocturnal Note"; inspired by the harmonies of heaven, it sings "darkling, and in shadiest Covert hid" (III, 39–40). It is at one with the benevolent order of nature, its dwelling-place "sacred" and "sequesterd" like Adam's "shadie" bower. It is the interpreter of the conflict in the poem because in the body it can pursue its flight "Through utter and through middle darkness borne" (III, 16) up to the fields of light and, in the mysterious and invisible world of the spirit, the "shadiest Covert," it can apprehend the meaning of its flight.

The conflict which the bird sees in the world of the poem between darkness and light is experienced by the bard in his own inner world as the contrast between blindness and vision. By his physical blindness he is "Cut off" from the circling alternations of light and dark which herald the "sweet approach of Ev'n or Morn" (III, 42), but by his spiritual illumination he can penetrate "Cleer Spring, or shadie Grove, or Sunnie Hill" (III, 28), the secret and sacred places of the true pastoral world.

This is the world which we lose in the poem with Adam's loss of the "shades" of Eden or Eve's loss of the "veil" of innocence. But as the blind bard's loss of eyesight is redeemed by his gift of vision, the loss of Eden is redeemed for Adam and Eve by the promise of the "Paradise within." In the vision of the future granted Adam by Michael, the eclipses which symbolize the shattering of nature's wheel are replaced by the rainbow, emblem of the continuance of the benevolent circular order of the universe:

> . . . Day and Night,
> Seed time and Harvest, Heat and hoary Frost

Shall hold thir course, till fire purge all things new,
Both Heav'n and Earth, wherein the just shall dwell.

(XI, 898–901)

This is not the seasonless round of unfallen nature which Adam and Eve knew in Eden, for in the mortal world the passing of time is marked by extremes of "Heat and hoary Frost," and by men's necessary labors. Yet these labors have their rewards on earth — "Seed time" shall have its "Harvest" — and when this earth shall have passed away, they will have their reward in the Paradise to come. In history as in nature, God will bring "Light out of darkness" (XII, 473) and the blindness of the first Adam shall be redeemed by the light of the second Adam:

> . . . so he dies,
> But soon revives, Death over him no power
> Shall long usurp; ere the third dawning light
> Returne, the Starres of Morn shall see him rise
> Out of his grave, fresh as the dawning light,
> Thy ransom paid, which Man from death redeems . . .

(XII, 419–424)

These lines, like the closing passage of *Lycidas*, transmute the images of the true pastoral nature which we lost by Adam's Fall into the triumphant images of Christianity, images of an order which finally transcends that nature because it transcends the possibility of loss, of death, of change.

In the great world envisioned in *Paradise Lost* and in the inner world of the narrator whose vision the poem is, conflict is resolved within unity, as light is brought out of darkness. In the structure of the poem which imitates the argument, contrast is finally included within the circular pattern of repetition. The tone of the narrator as he describes the banishment of Adam and Eve from Eden allows us to feel the restoration of order which we have seen shattered in the course of the poem. The shape of the epic returns to the pattern of the circle. The painful restoration of peace in the inner world of Adam and Eve in the closing lines repeats the cycle with which the poem opens. The triumphant pattern of God's will is the triumphant vision of Milton's narrator, recreated in the epic structure of *Paradise Lost*.

CONCLUSION

When Milton recreated *Adam unparadiz'd* into *Paradise Lost* he could not simply transpose dramatic scenes into narrative form. He had to invent a narrator capable of telling his story in a manner expressive of its meaning. The commonly accepted tradition that Moses was the inspired author of Genesis would have made him the most obvious choice for such a narrator,[1] and indeed in his earliest outline for a drama about the Fall of man, Milton intended to have the "invisible" world of innocence presented to his fallen audience by Moses. Yet in the epic Milton chose to ignore that tradition, to reject that narrator, inventing instead a special voice designed to express his special interpretation of the story of Adam's Fall. That narrative voice, as bird and especially as blind bard, is perhaps Milton's most brilliant creation. It gives to *Paradise Lost* its remarkable completeness. Everything in the poem is contained within the circle of the narrator's vision, and it is the scope, the inclusiveness, and the complexity of that vision which gives the epic its scope, inclusiveness, and complexity. It is also the nature of the narrator and his characteristic tone of voice which creates the impression we have when we read *Paradise Lost* of the poem's absolute uniqueness. There is no other speaker in English literature who stands in the same relation to his characters and his readers, no voice which uses quite the tone sustained throughout Milton's epic.

Just as the omnipresence of the narrator prevents us from reading *Paradise Lost* as a play, the nature of the speaker and his role prevent us from reading the epic as we are accustomed to read a novel.[2] The relation among narrator, characters, and reader in the English novel is traditionally social. The style in which we are addressed as readers of fiction echoes, at the same time that it may also criticize, our daily speech; the language of narration bears some relation to realistic idiom. The tone of the speaker in the novel is measured by our social modes of private conversation or of public discourse.

Milton in *Paradise Lost* avoids either of these large possibilities because the relation of the speaker to his characters and his readers is not social, and therefore his language could not be either the language of private conversation or of public speech. The speaker is "from the chearful waies of men/ Cut off" by his blindness. He is specifically excluded from our society by his special suffering and his special gift, which enable him to penetrate the surface of our fragmentary lives to a vision of essential, eternal relationships, of the circular order of God's universe. His language must therefore strip itself of purely local detail, of private associations and sense impressions, of conversational tones, of social contexts.

His is a personal language in the sense that it expresses the emotions of a fallen human being who sees and shares the sufferings of all men. Yet in another sense it is an impersonal language with the impersonality of a natural force, of a bird-song rising from the dark recess of the "shadiest Covert." It has the power and compression of private prayer, yet it is addressed to all men, with the conviction that we will share the speaker's great concerns. It is a unique language because its reference is both historical and psychological, its application both universal and individual, its pitch heroic, its intensity lyrical, its tone a beautiful mingling of judgment and sympathy. Such a fusion of qualities is possible only to a narrator who is fallen but redeemed like the blind bard, a creature limited like the bird but capable of flight and endowed with the power of heavenly song. This tone expresses in the voice of the narrator Milton's vision of the inner life of every man in its eternal relation to nature, to history, and to God.

NOTES

Foreword

1. For a recent analysis of the controversy see Bernard Bergonzi, "Criticism and the Milton Controversy," *The Living Milton*, ed. Frank Kermode (London, 1960), pp. 162–180.

2. In his revaluation of Milton, T. S. Eliot emphasized Milton's unique poetic "mastery" and "control." See "Milton," *Milton Criticism*, ed. James Thorpe (London, 1956), p. 324.

Introduction. The Question of Meaning

1. John Milton, "The Reason of Church Government Urged Against Prelaty," *The Student's Milton*, ed. F. A. Patterson (New York, 1947), pp. 525–526. All quotations from Milton's prose and poetry are taken from this edition.

2. Studies effective in this re-education are: C. M. Bowra, *From Virgil to Milton* (London, 1957); Douglas Bush, *Paradise Lost in Our Time* (Ithaca, N. Y., 1945); C. S. Lewis, *A Preface to Paradise Lost* (London, 1954).

3. Some relationships between Milton's style and Scriptural accommodation have been discussed recently by Roland Frye, *God, Man and Satan* (Princeton, 1960).

4. "Subjects for Poems and Plays from the Cambridge Manuscript," *Student's Milton*, p. 1129.

5. See especially William Haller, *The Rise of Puritanism* (New York, 1938), and Maurice Kelley, *This Great Argument* (Princeton, 1941).

6. "Reason of Church Government," *Student's Milton*, p. 525.

7. See for example John Peter, *A Critique of Paradise Lost* (New York, 1960), p. 11: "Poetry's task being to convey, not to assert, we should prefer to see this, instead of being told"; A. J. A. Waldock, *Paradise Lost and Its Critics* (Gloucester, Mass., 1959), p. 78: "in any imaginative work at all it is the demonstration, by the very nature of the case, that has the higher validity: an allegation can possess no comparable authority."

8. Among the first to argue this approach were: John Erskine, "The Theme of Death in *Paradise Lost*," *PMLA*, XXXII (1917),

573–582; J. H. Hanford, "The Dramatic Element in *Paradise Lost*," *SP*, XIV (1917), 178–195; E. E. Stoll, "Was Paradise Well Lost?", *PMLA*, XXXIII (1918), 429–435.

9. *The Spectator*, No. 369, ed. G. G. Smith (London, 1925), III, 197.

10. Edward Phillips, "The Life of Mr. John Milton," *Student's Milton*, p. xl.

11. See for example Waldock, *Paradise Lost and Its Critics*, p. 49.

12. "The Marriage of Heaven and Hell," *The Complete Writings of William Blake*, ed. Geoffrey Keynes (New York, n.d.), p. 150: "The reason Milton wrote in fetters when he wrote of Angels and God, and at liberty when of Devils & Hell, is because he was a true Poet and of the Devil's party without knowing it."

13. Much of Book VI seems to me to be inferior to the rest of the poem, perhaps because concrete and abstract realities are not metaphorically identified as they are elsewhere in the poem. This identification by sacred metaphor is discussed especially in Chapter IV.

Chapter I. Tone — The Bird and the Blind Bard

1. Addison, *Spectator*, No. 297, II, 177; Samuel Johnson, "Life of Milton," *Lives of the English Poets* (London, 1950), I, 103. The relation of these epic introductions to the total poem is argued from different points of view by R. W. Condee, "The Formalized Openings of Milton's Epic Poems," *JEGP*, L (1951), 502–508; John Diekhoff, "The Function of the Prologues in *Paradise Lost*," *PMLA*, LVII (1942), 697–704; F. J. Pequigney, "*Paradise Lost*, Epic of Inwardness," Harvard University, unpublished dissertation (1959), ch. iv.

2. This allusion is discussed by Jackson Cope, "Milton's Muse in *Paradise Lost*," *MP*, LV (1957), 6–10.

3. "Areopagitica," *Student's Milton*, p. 750. See also pp. 733, 748, 751, 752.

4. My indebtedness will be evident here and throughout this book to ideas suggested by William Empson, *Some Versions of Pastoral* (Norfolk, Conn., n.d.), pp. 149–191.

5. For a discussion of Milton's treatment of the legend of Eden as true myth see Isabel MacCaffrey, *Paradise Lost as "Myth"* (Cambridge, Mass., 1959).

6. It has been pointed out that Milton is here freely paraphrasing Virgil. See Bush, *Paradise Lost in Our Time*, p. 104.

7. For the identification and now classic discussion of this doctrine see A. O. Lovejoy, "Milton and the Paradox of the Fortunate Fall," *ELH*, IV (1937), 161–179.

Chapter II. Point of View and Comment

1. This and similar devices are mentioned but not discussed in detail by Frank Kermode, "Adam Unparadised," *Living Milton*, pp. 85–123.

2. See for example Waldock, *Paradise Lost and Its Critics*, pp. 49, 78, 81.

3. See for example D. C. Allen, *The Harmonious Vision* (Baltimore, 1954), p. 104; Empson, *Some Versions of Pastoral*, p. 189; Kermode, "Adam Unparadised," p. 106.

4. For an entirely different reading and evaluation of the scene see Waldock, *Paradise Lost and Its Critics*, pp. 42–56.

5. Milton's allusions to Homer in this passage are discussed by Bush, *Paradise Lost in Our Time*, p. 105.

Chapter III. Simile and Catalogue

1. Allen, *Harmonious Vision*, p. xi.

2. For discussions of Milton's similes see the articles by James Whaler: "Animal Simile in *Paradise Lost*," *PMLA*, XLVII (1932), 534–553; "The Compounding and Distribution of Simile in *Paradise Lost*," *MP*, XXVIII (1931), 313–327; "Grammatical *Nexus* of the Miltonic Simile," *JEGP*, XXX (1931), 327–334; "The Miltonic Simile," *PMLA*, XLVI (1931), 1034–1074.

Chapter IV. Sacred Metaphor

1. *The Poetical Works of Edmund Spenser*, ed. J. C. Smith and E. de Selincourt (London, 1948), p. 140. Other quotations from Spenser are taken from this edition.

2. Milton's discussion in *The Christian Doctrine* of the Fall of Adam and Eve shows the strength of Pauline influence in doctrine and language: "for even such as were not then born are judged and condemned in them, so that without doubt they also sinned in them,

and at the same time with them. Undoubtedly therefore all sinned in Adam. For Adam being the common parent and head of all, it follows that, as in the convenant, that is, in receiving the command-ment of God, so also in the defection from God, he either stood or fell for the whole human race . . ." *Student's Milton,* p. 997.

3. *Student's Milton,* p. 738.

4. Milton's practice of using words with both concrete and ab-stract meanings is discussed by MacCaffrey, *Paradise Lost as "Myth,"* especially pp. 65ff., 102, 109; W. B. C. Watkins, *An Anatomy of Mil-ton's Verse* (Baton Rouge, 1955), pp. 15f.

5. Certain misreadings of the poem have been encouraged, I be-lieve, by the tendency of modern critics to attribute their own dis-belief in the physical reality of Hell to Milton. See for example J. B. Broadbent, "Milton's Hell," *ELH,* XXI (1954), p. 170: The tor-ments of Hell "might be read as symbols of internal misery; but the strain in the verse and its rather more casual manner suggest that Milton is irritated at having to support the more sophisticated and Christian notion of an inner hell with the classico-medieval flames and sulphur."

6. Certain manipulations of diction and syntax analysed in this chapter are discussed from different points of view by F. T. Prince, *The Italian Element in Milton's Verse* (Oxford, 1954), pp. 105–131; MacCaffrey, *Paradise Lost as "Myth,"* pp. 98–118.

7. Empson, *Some Versions of Pastoral,* pp. 158f.

8. This important notion needs no elaboration here because it has been discussed at length by Arnold Stein, *Answerable Style* (Minne-apolis, 1953), pp. 75ff.

9. Kester Svendsen, *Milton and Science* (Cambridge, Mass., 1956), pp. 111f.

10. MacCaffrey, *Paradise Lost as "Myth,"* p. 106.

11. E. M. W. Tillyard, *The Miltonic Setting* (London, 1947), pp. 138f.

Chapter V. Allegory and Parody

1. Irene Samuel, *Plato and Milton* (Ithaca, 1947), p. 121.

2. For remarks about this passage see Waldock, *Paradise Lost and Its Critics,* p. 78; Stein, *Answerable Style,* p. 124.

3. "Life of Milton," p. 109. Italics mine.

4. Allan H. Gilbert, *On the Composition of Paradise Lost* (Chapel Hill, 1947), p. 162.

5. David Daiches, *Milton* (London, 1957), p. 176.

6. For connections between Satan and allegory see the remarks of Basil Willey, *The Seventeenth-Century Background* (New York, 1950), pp. 251f., 256f.

7. For objections to Milton's treatment of Satan see Waldock, *Paradise Lost and Its Critics*, pp. 65–96. In order to expand an alternative reading it has been necessary here to repeat briefly some ideas made familiar by other writers on Milton, especially Lewis, *Preface to Paradise Lost*, pp. 92ff.

8. For brief remarks about the allegorization of Satan see Stein, *Answerable Style*, pp. 157f.

9. "Areopagitica," *Student's Milton*, p. 738.

Chapter VI. Vision as Structure

1. MacCaffrey, *Paradise Lost as "Myth,"* p. 50.

2. See Marjorie H. Nicolson, "Milton and the Telescope," *ELH*, II (1935), 1–32.

3. M. M. Mahood, *Poetry and Humanism* (London, 1950), p. 177.

4. For a discussion of the traditional symbolism of the circle see Marjorie H. Nicolson, *The Breaking of the Circle* (Evanston, 1950).

5. For analysis of Milton's use of the word "all" see William Empson, *The Structure of Complex Words* (Norfolk, Conn., n.d.), pp. 101–104.

6. Mahood, *Poetry and Humanism*, p. 186.

7. Allen, *Harmonious Vision*, p. 104.

Conclusion

1. Arnold Williams, *The Common Expositor* (Chapel Hill, 1948), p. 24.

2. It has recently been suggested that Waldock's objections to *Paradise Lost* are the result of his assumption that it should be read as we read a novel. See Bergonzi, "Criticism and the Milton Controversy," pp. 177ff. I would add only that Waldock assumes both the novel and the epic should be fully *dramatized* in their presentation of the inner lives of their characters.